learn to **pray**

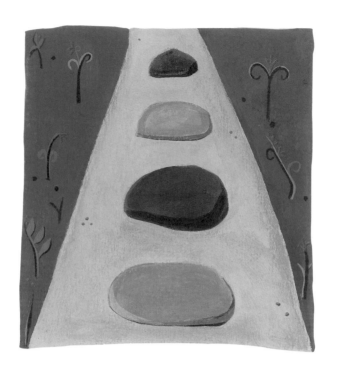

learn to
pray

A Practical Guide to Faith and Inspiration

Marcus Braybrooke

CHRONICLE BOOKS
SAN FRANCISCO

Learn to Pray
Marcus Braybrooke

First published in the United States in 2001 by Chronicle Books.

Conceived, created, and designed by
Duncan Baird Publishers Ltd.
Sixth Floor, Castle House
75–76 Wells Street, London W1T 3QH

Typeset in Apollo MT
Printed in Singapore

Library of Congress Cataloging-in-Publication Data available.

ISBN: 0-8118-3122-1

Cover illustrations: Tiffany Lynch

Distributed in Canada by
Raincoast Books
9050 Shaughnessy Street
Vancouver, B.C. V6P 6E5

10 9 8 7 6 5 4 3 2 1

Chronicle Books LLC
85 Second Street
San Francisco, CA 94105

www.chroniclebooks.com

NOTES
The abbreviations CE and BCE are used throughout this book:
CE Common Era (the equivalent of AD)
BCE Before the Common Era (the equivalent of BC)

To Rachel, a loving daughter
and a caring mother.
"A mother's care mirrors the
love of the divine."

Contents

introduction

Journalist Scott Bowles of *USA Today* has described a surprising first encounter with prayer. Seriously ill in hospital after a kidney transplant, he was understandably frightened. He shut himself in the bathroom so that his roommate would not see what he was doing, and prayed – although he did not know how to do this or whom to address. Soon afterward the doctors told him that his condition could be treated. For some, prayer brings healing, for others – as we shall see later in *Learn to Pray* – it delivers comfort or strength to cope with difficulty.

This book is for those who have never prayed and do not know how to start. But it is also for those who have experimented with prayer and who are seeking fresh perspectives and approaches to invigorate their prayer life. *Learn to Pray* provides straightforward advice on how to begin praying and gives clear explanations of why prayer is valuable. The insights and exercises are designed to help you find your own way of praying, to discover your own vision of the divine force to whom we pray.

Most books on prayer are written from the standpoint of one religious community. *Learn to Pray* attempts something new and different, seeking to be universal – to speak to members of all faiths and of none. There are many paths of prayer and each religious community has its established practices. As a Christian I have been shaped by that faith, but through worshipping alongside members of other traditions I have learned that prayer can be

a powerful unifying force. I hope this book will encourage mutual understanding among those who follow different spiritual paths.

Preparing this book has been at once challenging, enriching and humbling. Challenging, because many contemporaries reject or ignore the possibility of prayer and because I know that each reader will bring to the subject his or her own experience – often very different from mine. Enriching, because the book has led me to reflect deeply on the vital human activity of prayer and to join in the company of faithful people of many countries, religions and historical ages. Humbling, because *Learn to Pray* has made me newly aware that whether we are long-term travellers in faith or are just starting out, we are all no more than beginners in the great life adventure of coming to know the divine through prayer.

The Dawn of Understanding

Chapter One

Prayer, like plugging in an electrical appliance or logging on to the Internet, is a way of connecting. We may not understand how electricity or the World Wide Web work, but we still benefit from using them. Likewise, when we pray we may not at first understand to whom we are praying, nor how we might be answered, but by daring to make the connection we can access a reservoir of energy and understanding that is buried within us.

We do not need to use traditional religious approaches – to kneel, to clasp our hands, or to visit temples, synagogues, mosques or churches. We do not even need to speak of God. If we can see that there is more to life than meets the eye, that we can achieve more than merely the satisfaction of our senses or our material ambitions, then we have already taken the important first step. Our prayer life will soon begin to grow and deepen inside us, as we discover the resources that lie within – a bottomless well of love and affirmation.

the value of prayer

More things are wrought by prayer than this world dreams of.

ALFRED, LORD
TENNYSON
(1809–1892)

"**P**rayer," wrote the English novelist Iris Murdoch (1919–1999), "is the most essential of all human activities." We need prayer. By making it part of our daily routine, we can contact our true selves, learn to understand what we really, deeply want – and establish connections with others and with the world at large. Before we embark upon our spiritual journey, it is encouraging to enumerate some of the benefits prayer can bring to our lives.

In a world that pressures us to do everything at speed, prayer is a productive way to slow down. Pausing for a few minutes of prayer each day gives us the chance to review our deepest yearnings. Travelling into our inner selves, we gain confidence in our own resources, and discover a strength greater than our own. The self-knowledge and confidence that prayer brings can be a powerful help when we have to deal with misfortune or self-doubt. We can gain perspective on, say, a family argument, and see that our deepest selves are resilient, unaffected by such difficulties. In a crisis such as a serious illness we may find that prayer puts us in touch with therapeutic energies we only partly understand.

Prayer can also bind us together with others. Simply saying a brief prayer together before a meal, for example, expressing gratitude for the food we are about to enjoy and for each other's company, can help reinforce a sense of fellowship or kinship. Prayer can make us more sympathetic to others' predicaments – when we pray for other people we imaginatively put ourselves in their

place, and our goodness is enlarged as this happens. By encouraging our sympathy for others, prayer moves our attention away from what divides us and toward what unites us. Think of someone who has recently annoyed or offended you. Do you think you could forgive him or her? Sitting quietly, visualize the person, then think of five ways in which you are alike and five things that you would both enjoy doing. Imagine yourself expressing your forgiveness by offering a prayer – could you do this?

Many people who have experimented with prayer report that it brings them to a sense of harmony with all people and – in a spirit of thanksgiving – with nature. If we are all united, then we all share responsibility for the state of the world, and by following prayer's guide and modifying our behaviour, we can all effect change. Prayer is nothing less than an instrument for the transformation of the world. As a Chinese prayer puts it, "Change the world and begin with me."

pray as you can, not as you can't

As I began to write this, a squirrel ran up our drive, stretched itself out and started to sunbathe. I watched with riveted attention, admiring the squirrel's self-possession and vitality in repose. A line by the poet Gerard Manley Hopkins (1844–1889) echoed in my mind – "What I do is me, for that I came." Was that prayer? I do not know and I doubt whether it matters. For a few moments my spirit was uplifted. There are hundreds of definitions of prayer, and there is no right way to pray. As an old adage puts it, "Pray as you can, not as you can't."

We do not want to be beginners, but let us be convinced that we will never be anything else but beginners all our life.

THOMAS MERTON
(1915–1968)

The first step in learning to pray is to free ourselves from preconceptions of what prayer is. Perhaps childhood memories of being forced to say prayers have put us off for years; we may not believe in God; or we may doubt whether prayer has any effect. It is important not to feel anxious about such thoughts – they need not prevent us from finding our own way of praying, and they often fade as we discover the peace that prayer can bring. We should never be discouraged from embarking on our adventure. We are never too young or too old to benefit from learning to pray.

The second step on the road to prayer is to forget any fixed ideas we may have about *how* to pray. We do not need to worry whether we use words or keep quiet, whether we kneel down or sit or stand, whether we place our hands together or hold prayer beads. We can pray at any time, anywhere, in any way. The only prerequisite for prayer is that we be ourselves.

exercise one

liberate your spirit

It is possible to pray at any moment of the day, whatever your state of mind, but you will be able to express your prayer better, and find it more enriching, if you are relaxed and your mind is uncluttered. This simple exercise will help you to sweep away the day-to-day anxieties that crowd your thoughts, leaving you feeling calm and uplifted.

1. Sit comfortably and relax by tensing then releasing your muscles. Take a long, deep breath and slowly exhale, imagining that any remaining tension in your body is being set free with your out-breath. Try to empty your mind of all thoughts.

2. Close your eyes and picture a bird flying lazily across a clear blue sky. The bird is at one with itself and, as it responds to the gentle breeze, at one with nature. It dips low and then soars high into the vastness of blue.

3. Now imagine that you are that flying bird. You have no cares or worries – there are no restrictions, no fears and no painful memories to hold you back. You are completely free, entirely alive in the present moment, as you fly toward the sun.

4. You begin to soar effortlessly, ever higher and higher. Think of yourself as a lark ascending, singing out with limitless joy in harmony with the turning world, with the deep blue sky and its tall clouds, with life itself.

15

the light within

When asked how they imagined God, most people who responded to a recent survey came close to the predictable child's view, of "an old man with a long white beard up in the sky". It is not surprising that many of them also said that they did not believe in God. The image of a bearded heavenly father popularized in the works of European artists over the past thousand years is at odds with the modern scientific view of the universe. We now know that we live on a ball of rock spinning through space around the Sun, and many of us can no longer believe in a father God who sits in the blue sky above us. If prayer is to become real for us, our best starting point may be to look within ourselves rather than to gaze up at heaven.

To look directly at ourselves in this way, we will certainly have to penetrate layers of obfuscation. Many of us are so busy and distracted that we live only at a superficial level. In a world dominated by advertising and secular role models, we may be, to some extent, leading the lives that others make for us. Aware that we are not being our true selves, we may nevertheless give way to the pressures of others' expectations. Prayer is an opportunity to withdraw from the superficial level of peer pressure and travel down into the depths of our being.

When you have the chance, try this imaginative exercise – if possible, do it after reading this paragraph. Put the book aside and sit quietly with your eyes closed. Imagine diving deep down into your inner being. Go down, below your physical requirements, your mental activities, your emotional and social needs, to a place at the centre where all is still and you are your essential self without images or pretences. What do you find there?

In everyday life you may feel that you have many different selves – the you at work; the you at home with your husband, wife or partner, your children or your parents; the you who dreams of a better future; the you who seems to have difficulty shaking off the burden of the past. Throughout history experimenters with prayer – from Hindu sages in Ancient India more than 4,000 years ago to George Fox (1624–1691), the Englishman who founded the Society of Friends (now often called the Quakers), and others more recently – have reported that when you quiet the clamour of these many selves you discover deep within your being an inner witness or true self that is immortal, even divine. Fox, who was steeped in the Christian tradition, called this the inner light and identified it with the spirit of Christ – he said that he had experienced the living Christ "experimentally, without the help of any man, book or writing". The Indian sages called the inner core or self the *Atman* and said that it was no different from *Brahman*, the divinity who they believed had powered the creation of the universe and now sustained it.

Your decision to learn to pray offers you the chance to embark on the great adventure of discovering and coming to know your

I have spoken of a light in the soul that is uncreated and uncreatable.

MEISTER
ECKHART
(1260–1328)

inner self. Call it what you like: your deathless soul, your spirit, your higher self, your spiritual nature. You may or may not believe that it is an aspect of God, of the One, a precious fragment of the Consciousness that animates all life. You may see it as your conscience. For now let us call it, like Fox, your "inner light". Living with it is at once both the hardest and the most rewarding challenge of your life. It is an ally, a guide, a source of strength, yet also a firm taskmaster, calling you to live up to your highest ideals.

Adjusting to the inner light may require changes in your way of living. Some people have felt the light commanding them to opt out of the "rat race" – perhaps to abandon a status-driven career path in favour of work that embodies their convictions about what really matters. More modestly, following the inner light leads to a simple change of attitude, a slowing down of pace – for example, making fewer commitments so that we are not always in a rush and have time to pray, time to listen to others and help them, time to do everything to the best of our ability.

If you commute to work, do you travel glumly and see other travellers as a nuisance? Do you spend so much energy worrying about the day ahead that you are not living in the present? When you arrive at work, do you greet your colleagues in a rush and scarcely listen to their reply? A little time regularly spent in prayer can correct such errors of perspective by making us more aware of what we should truly value. Prayer is the best use of five minutes, deepening our sense of all the rest of the time we have at our disposal, guiding us in how to use that time most rewardingly.

The Self of all beings, living within the body, is eternal and cannot be harmed.

THE BHAGAVAD GITA
(HINDU SCRIPTURE)

exercise two

start your inner sunrise

Our concern with artificial, socially determined goals sometimes threatens to dominate our lives. We may be so driven by a desire to keep up with friends, colleagues or family that we no longer bother to consider what we believe, deep down, to be the right path. This exercise leads you to an encounter with your true self or inner light through prayer – a wonderful dawning into a new world of personal truth.

1. Settle yourself comfortably with pen and paper. Now recall your hopes for yourself, perhaps when you left school or college, when you married or started a family. Can you remember the person you wanted to be?

2. Ask yourself whether you have lived up to these hopes. If you think you have fallen short, write down why you think you did so, then note a few ways in which you would like to change in the future.

3. Pause for a moment and visualize how you would like to be. Be confident in the knowledge that you can achieve this if your desire for inner change is strong enough. You have the capacity to be transformed by boundless power and resources that are locked within you and ready to be released as you require them. You need only decide to make a new start and then persevere, even in the face of the difficulties that are likely to cross your path – as they cross the paths of all of us.

19

what do we call god?

No words can adequately describe the higher reality many of us call "God". It is a good idea to experiment – to try out different ways of addressing the transcendent spirit. What matters is to choose a word that makes sense for you.

Christian and Jewish prayers often refer to "the Lord", but some people may dislike this because of its association with feudal power structures. Many of us like to use adjectives such as "Immortal" or "Invisible", names devised on the basis of what God is not and therefore implying that divine reality is beyond description. Some Buddhists talk of divine "Emptiness", while Hindus say "*Neti, Neti*" (God is "Not this, Not that") – for although Hindus revere many different gods and offer their devotions to vividly sculpted images of them, they see them all as faces of a single sustaining divinity. Muslims speak of the ninety-nine names of God, which include "the Shaper", "the Just" and "the Protector".

You may decide to speak in personal terms, such as "Father" or "Mother", because these words suggest that life is a gift and that we are cared for. Or, to reflect greater intensity of feeling, you may prefer a name such as "Beloved" or "Lover of my soul". Such words as "Father", Mother" or "Lover" are intended to be useful as metaphors – they do not suggest that the reality we address in our prayers is in essence either female or male, and neither do they suggest that the divine being has physical attributes. Their usefulness is that they express an intimate relationship.

By what name shall I call upon you, who are beyond all name? All names are given to you and yet none can comprehend you. How shall I call you then, O you, the Beyond-all name?

GREGORY OF NAZIANZEN (c.329–390CE)

Focusing on God as the voice of wisdom, you might feel comfortable with "Teacher" or "Guide". Or you might choose a more elevated name such as "the Real", "the Source of Life" or "the Spring of Truth". You might address the "Self" (equating God with the inner light) or "the One" (the unifying spirit), while "Lord of Love" or "Lord of Life" express humility and gratitude. Then again, you might find that any name gets in the way and it is best just to be quiet – God's first name is sometimes said to be silence.

be still

Just over a hundred years ago, the French author Charles Péguy, to the annoyance of many readers, published a long poem about Joan of Arc with a number of pages that were entirely blank. The reason, he explained, was to give the reader "time to think". We need blank pages in our lives. When we make time to pray, we are creating a pocket of stillness amid the rush and hubbub, a precious place in which we can be truly ourselves, where we can listen to our inner voice, focus on our inner light.

"Be still" is the first rule of prayer. It is more difficult than it sounds. Try sitting still for five minutes – how many times do you have an urge to scratch, or cross and uncross your legs? What is going on inside your head? Are you mentally writing the minutes of your last conversation? Are you wondering what to cook for supper? Some people find inner stillness is easier when they are walking, because the rhythmic motion appears to soothe the mind.

I have seen many who were saved by silence but none who were saved by chatter.

ST AMBROSE
(340–397CE)

It might help you to find a favourite place, away from noise and distraction, but you can practise stillness anywhere. You might be queueing in the post office or waiting for the kettle to boil. Instead of growing impatient, put the time to use. Breathe deeply. To give your mind something to focus on, you might inwardly recite a prayer you have memorized – perhaps one from this book. Go through it in your mind, giving your full attention to each word. Already you are praying, and you have only just started to learn how! It is easier than you thought.

exercise three

find an inner sanctuary

Tranquil places in which we feel close to nature are particularly conducive to prayer. Sadly, few of us have access to these soothing oases during our busy day-to-day existence. This exercise enables you to create a sanctuary in your mind's eye and then carry it with you so that you can visit it whenever you want to pray – even if you are in the middle of a crowded store or travelling in a car, bus, train, ferry or plane.

1. Spend a few minutes listening to your breathing. Inhale and exhale slowly and deeply. This helps to relax the body and quieten the mind.

2. When you feel relaxed, think of a place you know well in which you feel at one with nature. If you find it hard to choose a familiar place, create an imaginary one – perhaps a sandy beach, the grassy bank of a gurgling stream, or the gentle sweep of a hillside.

3. See yourself sitting alone in the place you have pictured. Recreate as many details of the landscape as you can. What are the colours around you? What are the smells and sounds? Are you being warmed by the sun or gazing at a starry night sky?

4. Imagine that you feel completely at peace with your surroundings – an ideal state of mind for prayer. Practise this exercise regularly until you can conjure up at will this image and its accompanying sensations.

23

promise and commitment

After listening to a recital, you may decide you want to learn to play the piano. But you don't expect simply to sit down and play like a maestro; you know you will have to practise, regularly setting aside time to develop your skills. Learning to pray is no different. You need to make a promise to yourself that you will practise stillness and communing with your inner self.

Prayer is about exploring a relationship with your true self. If you arrive for a romantic dinner and find that for the second time in a week your date has not turned up, you are likely to think that he or she is just a flirt and is not serious about you. It is a waste of your time to flirt with your inner self. Make a commitment in good faith to practise prayer if you want to enjoy its rewards.

St Paul wrote to the early Christians in Galatia, "As a man sows, so shall he reap." If you sow violence, you reap violence; but equally if you act with love, you are more likely to receive love. By committing to prayer and praying regularly you are preparing the ground in which a harvest of love can grow: day by day you will develop your relationship with your inner self and come closer to integrating what you do with what you deeply want.

Your inner light is the most faithful friend you can imagine. It harbours resources powerful enough to transform your life and to flood out through you as a force for peace in the lives of those around you. You have to do some of the work yourself. Stick to it, and your inner friend will not let you down.

Ask and it will be given you; search, and you will find; knock, and the door will be opened for you.

JESUS,
MATTHEW 7: 7

24

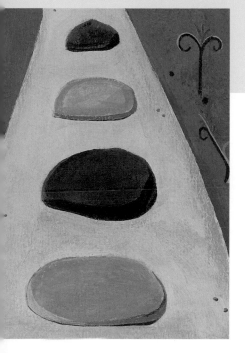

exercise four

commit to prayer

A sportsman or sportswoman determined to win a medal or trophy first works out a detailed training schedule and makes a commitment covering diet and other lifestyle matters. This exercise provides an opportunity to get into training for prayer, to make some simple commitments to learning to pray.

1. Find a quiet corner and sit for a few moments with a piece of paper and pencil. Write down your commitments to prayer – this makes them more definite.

2. Allocate time to the practice of prayer. Be realistic. Could you manage ten minutes a day, or half an hour a week? Write down how much time you can spend.

3. Resolve to tell someone else that you are learning to pray – it will increase your determination to make your prayer life work. Maybe the person you tell will occasionally ask you how you are getting on. You will find this a great encouragement. Write down the name of the person you intend to tell.

4. Choose an added incentive to help you keep up your regular commitment. It does not need to be a major thing – for example, if you choose to pray for ten minutes in your lunchbreak, decide that, if you skip prayers then, you will also skip your mid-afternoon cup of tea.

awe and wonder

T he birth of a child is a miraculous event that can fill us with wonder as we witness the first moments of a new life. Many feel astonishment when they visit places of great beauty, such as the Grand Canyon or the Niagara Falls. For some a sense of awe comes in the wake of a bad accident or a brush with death. Experiences that remind us of our mortality, our smallness in a vast universe or the mysterious fact of our existence often prompt us to ponder the possibilities of a sacred dimension. Such experiences can prove a powerful impetus to prayer.

Awe-inspiring moments can be life-changing. The British explorer Francis Younghusband (1863–1942) said that in the mountains of Tibet he felt "in touch with the flaming heart of the universe"; afterward he said, "Never again can I bear enmity," and

To see a world

in a grain

of sand

And a heaven in

a wild flower,

Hold infinity

in the palm of

your hand

And eternity

in an hour.

WILLIAM BLAKE
(1757–1827)

PRAYER: A NEW VISION

In contemplative prayer the English mystic Julian of Norwich (c.1342–c.1413) saw the entire creation in the form of a tiny hazelnut and understood that it could be sustained in that or any other form by the love of the divine. Just as with moments of wonder in our daily lives, such insights come unbidden. But if we commit ourselves to regular prayer our perceptions are transformed by intimacy with the divine – habitually we come to see our own selves and the world around us in a new light.

dedicated his life to the service of others. The power of such transformative moments comes partly from the way they arrive unannounced.

Even so, you can consciously open yourself up to the dimension beyond the material by putting yourself in special environments. You might go for a walk in a great wood, by a lake or in the mountains. It might be best to go alone, so that you can pause and be quiet when you wish; or you could travel with a friend or group of friends but make a pact of silence before you set out. If you are in a city, visit a museum or gallery that exhibits sacred art. Rather than trying to see everything, select two or three items and spend time contemplating them – perhaps a painting by El Greco or Titian, a statue of the Buddha or a Hindu sculpture such as the dancing form of Shiva known as Nataraja ("Lord of the Dance").

Perhaps you have experienced what poet T.S. Eliot (1888–1965) called "a moment in and out of time". Sit quietly and try to recall it. You can probably remember the exhilaration. If you can taste it again, savour it. Offer thanks to the power that made the experience available to you.

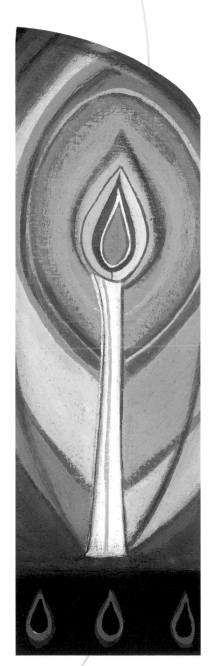

heart, mind and emotion

We might be prompted to pray by a rush of feelings – perhaps awe or gratitude or fear. However, we need to apply *understanding* to bring direction to our prayer life, to make it bear fruit for us. Prayer involves mind as well as heart, understanding as well as emotion.

To borrow an image from the Hindu scriptures, we might say that our progress in life is like that of a horse-drawn chariot. There is a charioteer, of course – our self. The horses are the strong impulses – the sensory experiences and emotions – that run through our bodies and brains. If left to their own devices, the horses would gallop off wildly. However, the chariot has not only a wise passenger – our inner light – but also a skilled charioteer – our understanding. Without control directed by a wise sense of purpose, our feelings, however positive, would take us far from where we have chosen to go. However, under firm direction the horses' energy is channelled into purposeful forward motion.

No doubt we have all at times let go of the reins and allowed our horses to follow their instincts. This is not disastrous if it is merely a temporary aberration. But as a way of life it can lead us into deep trouble. To use a more up-to-date image, it is to fly a two-engine plane on a single engine. However much fuel we have, we will either come down with a bump or fly pointlessly around in circles. Prayer is an opportunity for us to integrate emotions and understanding so that our flight is straight and smooth.

One of the difficulties we might have with these ideas is the problem of definitions. It might help, therefore, to offer some key distinctions. In contemplating the mind we sometimes think of intellect, but this is in fact a narrowly specialized function: you do not have to be intellectual to lead a rewarding life of prayer. More important is reason, which guarantees that

our thoughts and actions are well founded. Most important of all is understanding, combining mental and intuitive faculties. Taken far enough, understanding matures into wisdom — a progression for which prayer is a wonderful pathway.

It is worth thinking in similar ways about emotion. An emotion can pass through us like a tidal wave, leaving us at best disorientated, at worst in moral danger. That is because emotions flow from the same spring as pride, vanity, and so on. Yet to seal off our feelings entirely is to block compassion for other people — and to make prayer impossible. A useful rule of thumb is to distinguish the ego, which gives out negative feelings, from the heart, which gives out positive feelings. Follow the heart and the understanding: when you find them in prayer, like head lamps (to call upon yet another transport metaphor) they will light your way.

a different perspective

It can sometimes be difficult to get started with prayer. We can become paralyzed if we think too much about praying – and then we need a fresh perspective to restore our spontaneity. The *koans* or paradoxical statements used in meditation by some Zen Buddhists can be a jumping-off point into prayer.

Have you ever been so involved in doing something you loved that you forgot for a moment who and where you were? In complete concentration you lost your sense of a separate self. Zen Buddhism aims to produce this direct experience of the unity of all life, of the entire cosmos, by shattering conventional ways of thinking about our individuality. According to Zen practitioners, the puzzling koans "throw sand into the eyes of the intellect to force us to open our mind's eye".

Teachers of meditation, particularly in the Rinzai school of Zen, use koans to encourage novices to develop an intuitive rather than an intellectual response. Sit quietly in silence for a few moments and consider these well-known koans: "What is the sound of one hand clapping?" "What does your face look like before your parents' birth?" Or try these these less traditional koans: "What colour is air?" "What is the religion of water?" As you engage with these questions, do not be concerned that your intellect is baffled. You are learning the limitations of intellect – and perhaps at the same time glimpsing, however dimly, some kind of direct and profound truth that may help you in your prayer life.

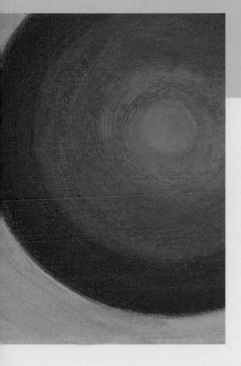

exercise five

smile in the moment

Zen emphasizes total concentration on the present moment, encouraging us to try to be intent on what we are doing, be it walking or cooking or arranging flowers. Thich Nhat Hahn, a Buddhist monk, has suggested that concentrating on smiling is a good way to foster a sense of alertness. This simple exercise may set you on the way to a more focused, concentrated state of mind that helps you to be mindful of the divine in all your daily activities.

1. Draw your lips into a faint, scarcely perceptible smile – the sort of smile that you see on images of the Buddha. To your surprise you may realize that much of the time you are in the habit of frowning.

2. Breathe in deeply: feel calm pass through your body. As you breathe out, smile. Concentrate on your breathing, on the present moment. Know it for what it is: a gift from the divine, a wonderful, vibrant instant.

3. Try to keep a smile on your face after finishing the exercise. Whatever you do next, concentrate on it – do not rush, or think of the next task. You will find even doing the dishes, say, or mending a bicycle puncture is more enjoyable if you are wholly alert. Be mindful of the presence of the divine as you work; offer each moment to the source of life as a prayer of gratitude.

31

qualities of the divine

Our father and mother

God is our father and mother,

and has shown mercy to me.

In peace I will walk on the straight road.

*Adapted from a prayer of the Cheyenne Native
North American tribe*

O clearness beyond measure

O burning mountain, O chosen sun,

O perfect moon, O fathomless well,

O unattainable height, O clearness beyond measure,

O wisdom without end, O mercy without limit,

O strength beyond resistance, O crown of all majesty,

The humblest of all you created sings your praise.

Mechtild of Magdeburg (1207–1294), German mystic

If I worship You

O my Lord ... if I worship you for your own sake,
withhold not from me your eternal beauty.

Rab'ia of Basra (c.713–801CE), Muslim mystic

I will sing you a song

O, Lord of the Universe I will sing you a song.
Where can you be found,
and where can you not be found?
Where I pass – there you are.
Where I remain – there, too, you are.
You, you and only you.

Hasidic Jewish song

Our Lord fills every heart

The Infinite is within as well as without.
Our Lord fills every heart.
He is the earth, the sky and the underworld;
he fills the entire universe.

Guru Arjan, Fifth Sikh Guru, 16th century

blessings

Two Gaelic blessings

Deep peace of the running wave to you,

deep peace of the flowing air to you,

deep peace of the quiet earth to you,

deep peace of the shining stars to you,

deep peace of the Son of Peace to you.

Prayer used by the Iona community, Scotland

May the road rise to meet you.

May the wind be always at your back.

May the sun shine warm upon your face.

May the rains fall softly upon your fields.

Until we meet again,

may God hold you in the hollow of his hand.

Ancient Gaelic blessing

Prayer for all beings

May creatures all abound in well-being and peace,

may all be blessed with peace always;

all creatures weak or strong,

all creatures great and small,

creatures unseen or seen,

dwelling afar or near,

born or awaiting birth,

may all be blessed with peace.

Sutta-Nipata (from the Buddhist Pali canon)

Those who hope in the Lord

Even youths grow tired and weary, and young
men stumble and fall, but those who hope in the
Lord will renew their strength. They will soar on
wings like eagles, they will run and not grow weary,
they will walk and not be faint.

Isaiah 40: 30–31

Dialogue with the Divine

Chapter Two

When you are having a conversation with a friend, you do not talk all the time — your listening, watching, smiling and touching may be as valuable to the communication between you as your words. In the same way, dialogue with the divine involves more than *saying* prayers. Learning to pray also involves learning to listen and to look for signs that the divine is active in your life. Prayer is a two-way communication.

Imagine a prayer line connecting you with the divine, the One, or whatever you wish to call it. To begin with you may find that you use the line only when in a crisis, but as you experience the value of the connection you will make contact more and more often. You will try out ways to keep the prayer line open; and you will remember to use the line to communicate gratitude and love as well as requests for help. In time you can even go beyond the need for conscious dialogue, to a state of joyful, silent union.

someone is listening

"**P**ray to God in any way you like," advised Hindu teacher Sri Ramakrishna (1836–1886). "God is sure to hear you, for God can hear even the footfall of an ant." The act of praying is never wasted: all sincere prayers have an effect. Part of the adventure of prayer is that the effects may be different from our expectation.

Prayers are answered in many ways. If we feel that a prayer has been ignored, perhaps this is because we cannot see or understand the answer. Remember that, enmeshed in daily life, we do not view the whole picture: we may initially see setbacks as denials of prayers, but months later see that the "denials" developed inner qualities in ourselves that we needed in our lives. Sometimes we have to accept that our prayers have not been answered in the way we hoped. Even in such cases, however, prayer benefits us and the objects of our prayers. Imagine a woman who prays that her uncle will recover from a life-threatening illness; he dies, but she hears that he was calm as he prepared for death. She feels comforted by the knowledge that her prayers eased his passage to the beyond.

Trust in your prayers. Try to pray with a firm belief that the prayer will be answered in one way or another – perhaps through the support of other people, in whom the divine also shines.

The prayer of a pure heart never goes unanswered.

MAHATMA
GANDHI
(1869–1948)

exercise six

see the arrow

Like a medieval outlaw's message attached to an arrow that flies through the air and thwacks into a tree, the answer to prayer may come in a way we would never have foreseen. This exercise encourages you to keep a broad look-out for signs that the divine light is shining in your life.

1. *Sit quietly and consider the past few weeks and months. Has some event or conversation made you wonder what your life is about? Why did you start to read this book?*

2. *Have you achieved something you believe your true inner self would be proud of? Conversely, is there something you found disappointing that in a wider perspective you can see was for the best?*

3. *Has something for which you were striving arrived by a different means than you expected? Could you have missed out on help because you were unprepared to accept it? Have you passed up an offer of support because it came from an unexpected source?*

4. *Visualize the divine light shining within you, directing help to you through unexpected, even secret channels — like the arrow shot from the impenetrable shadows — to let you know that support is there for you, that someone, some force is working for good on your behalf, perhaps despite appearances.*

asking

Many of us find it difficult to ask for help. We are encouraged to see self-reliance as a strength, and to believe that admitting our need for resources greater than our own to deal with a problem is a sign of inadequacy. But in truth to ask for help, both from other people and from the divine, is far from being inadequate – it is a sign that you have understood your difficulties and are taking postive action to address them. Buoyed up by prayer, you can move forward to deal effectively with any situation.

When we are afraid to ask for help, we grow used to muddling along. We shrink from focusing on our difficulties because to do so brings home that we are not coping. In this way some of us are sucked into spirals of debt or into patterns of damaging behaviour such as alcoholism or a drug habit. In such a life crisis, admitting that you need help is the first step on the road to recovery.

Deciding to learn to pray is a similarly decisive step, even if the problems we have may be less severe and less obvious than these examples. It marks the beginning of a new life in which we acknowledge that we are not each an isolated soul fending for itself, but part of a network of interactions with humanity, and with the divine through both our own spirit and the spirit of others – family, friends, colleagues, acquaintances, even strangers. Prayer – even when it has an element of asking – is an affirmation of our spiritually informed humanity. Our spiritual sincerity and faith give us the *right* to ask.

Anyone who feels uncomfortable about the prospect of asking, who can't help feeling that asking is not in the spirit of true prayer, that it is somehow not subtle enough for so mystical or spiritual an activity, would do well to think back to our childhood.

Our purest state of mind is a state close to innnocence, uncluttered by material ambition. Paradoxically, we may be experienced in the realities of suffering, or in the moral pitfalls in which people can so readily find themselves trapped, yet

still there is at the very centre of our being a spirit of uncomplicated goodness. Children, like adults, can lose this beneath a clutter of selfishness, but their approach to life is usually more innocent than adults can achieve in their daily lives. When a child speaks his or her first prayer – "Please, God, give me ..." – that child is being positive, open and trusting, rather than downcast and worried.

We all respond to the unaffected simplicity of well-behaved children. When you pray, imagine that you are tapping into your childhood self: scales of sophistication and complexity are falling from your inner self, leaving it pure and innocent.

Relax, and ask with natural, unaffected confidence. Just as, when you have insomnia, it does not help to try very hard to go to sleep, so you cannot use determination or willpower to reach an effective mental state for asking. The effectiveness of prayer does not depend on how hard you try: what matters is how directly and sincerely you express yourself.

It may help to imagine the divine as a deeply loving and concerned parent who is waiting to be asked for help. You do not need to impress him or her or to perform any unusual tricks – simply ask. If you can bring yourself to a sense of intimate connection with the divine, you will be in a suitably relaxed state of mind for asking in prayer. A good way to establish intimacy is slowly to repeat a name for the divine with which you feel comfortable. Try,

ASKING AND DOING

When you ask in prayer, you have to act in support of your asking. If you are unhappy at work and pray for a new job, scan the situations vacant and canvass actively for a new opening. Even when you pray for a vision, such as global peace, seek small-scale practical ways of making peace in your life and your sphere of influence. Commitment to action is an integral part of your prayer. Prayer gives you access to the divine, which brings you untold strength. But the matter cannot be surrendered from your hands. Even unexpected blessings depend on your actions – otherwise they are merely good luck.

perhaps, "Beloved", "Father" or "Mother". Some people recommend holding both hands over your heart as you do so, and imagining the warmth of the divine presence flooding in turn through your shoulders, arms, chest and stomach – and on through your entire body. When you sit down to ask in prayer, try spending a minute or two repeating the holy name. You will probably then find you can proceed to straightforward, unaffected asking.

Ask with confidence that your prayer will be answered and ask for what you really want. Do not make requests halfheartedly or tone them down because you do not believe they will be granted. One aspect of the self-knowledge that comes through prayer is the ability to see our wishes clearly and to distinguish between passing flights of fancy (or the grasping of the ego) and the deeply held desires of our true self. Once we have made the distinction, we should commit ourselves wholeheartedly to what we want. For our desire, our commitment – perhaps to changing ourselves, or to finding a practical expression, in our actions, of the words of our prayers – is the driving force of our asking.

Our confidence in our prayers will lead us to be receptive – to expect and accept help. Once this confidence is well established, we will not expect help to take the most obvious form. If we pray for some kind of fulfilment or release, it will not arrive the next day like a package by guaranteed mail. The divine spirit, working on behalf of our best intentions, will respond in terms of the most appropriate possible outcome. Your faith that this is so will be its own most obvious reward.

saying thank you

Next time you feel unhappy, try itemizing those aspects of your life for which you are grateful. They may include a safe place to live, a special friendship, the support of your family, good food to eat, the beauty of a landscape, even the warmth of the sun. Once you have performed this stocktaking, things may look a little brighter – so offer a short prayer of thanks. Gratitude is the apt response to the privilege of being alive in a universe suffused with the divine spirit – even when we have challenges to meet.

The worthy person is grateful and mindful of benefits done to him.

ANGUTTARA NIKAYA (BUDDHIST SCRIPTURE)

Hymns of thanksgiving are sung by people of most religions. Sadi, a thirteenth-century Muslim poet, spoke for many faiths when he declared, "I cannot draw a breath without gratitude to the Friend ... Praise be to the Lord, the giver of all good." In Dallas, Texas, the Center for World Thanksgiving, which organizes inter-faith prayer meetings and concerts, has found thanksgiving to be a powerful unifying bond between people of different religions.

Try to make time for a regular daily act of giving thanks. Even when it seems like a bad day, take a few minutes to recall good moments – the sparkle of sunshine on a wet street, the sympathetic assistance you received from a friend or a passer-by when something went wrong. As you think of people for whose love or help you are grateful, you might find that the act of thanksgiving becomes a prayer for them. If you give thanks each day for the life and love of your daughter, say, or your mother, you are holding her in the light of your own love and of the divine presence.

If we make a habit of giving thanks, we will find that our lives can be transformed by gratitude. As we become aware that there are more positive things in the routine of our lives than we had realized, we begin to see life as enriching – to see possibilities, not difficulties. The English Romantic poet William Wordsworth (1770–1850) wrote in a letter, "Gratitude is the handmaid to hope."

Gratitude arises naturally as we learn through our prayer dialogue to focus on what we truly value. If friends tell us to count our "blessings" we may be tempted to dismiss the advice as a pious pronouncement. But we must never shy away from the profound truths that piety often expresses. When we focus on our goals –

even our most cherished spiritual goals – we often forget about the gifts we already possess. It is easy to see the truth of this if we think about how much we would miss them if they were lost. Sadly, of course, this does indeed happen to many of us through bereavement, ill-health, and so on. In such cases it may take a great deal of time to learn how to give thanks retrospectively, for a blessing surrendered.

You that have given so much to me, Give one thing more – a grateful heart.

GEORGE HERBERT
(1593–1633)

Try imagining that you have been told you are losing your sight. Close your eyes and think about all the objects, views and faces you want to commit to memory. Picture yourself as a blind person going through your daily routine in darkness. Now open your eyes – you have been granted a reprieve and are thankfully gazing on the sights you thought would be denied to you for ever. This thankfulness is a form of prayer.

Being grateful is a shift of perspective, a recognition that not only health but life itself is a gift. You might be caring for a sick aunt and beginning to resent the loss of your freedom, but then you focus on the kindness she shows despite her illness and you feel gratitude that you are able to help her when she needs care. As you practise noticing the good things rather than the bad, thankfulness becomes instinctive. At the same time your sympathy for others is deepened. Compassion, Buddhism teaches, is generated by appreciation of our lot. To recognize that the good things we enjoy are gifts is to acknowledge that we have no absolute right to them. Thankfulness inspires us to pray and work for a more equitable sharing of the gifts of the world.

exercise seven

pray thankfully

Take a few minutes to think about what is good in your life. Each time you are able to answer "yes" to any of the questions in the exercise, pause for a moment. In your mind or out loud, say "thank you" to the divine. Make thanksgiving a regular part of your life and you will grow spiritually.

1. Think first about your body, forgetting for now any aches and pains you may have. Consider the following questions. Can you see? Can you hear? Can you walk? Are you well nourished and fit? Give thanks.

2. Think about the people with whom you have shared your life. Remember your childhood. Do you have fond memories of caring parents, grandparents, teachers or schoolfriends? Give thanks.

3. Let your thoughts turn to those around you today. Is your life enriched by a partner, children, colleagues, friends, or even a pet animal? Give thanks.

4. Think about all the things that bring you pleasure. Do you enjoy sport, cooking or eating a good meal, or walking in the park or in the country? Do you love the buzz of the city? Do you feel uplifted by your favourite music? Do you find pleasure and wisdom in your reading? Give thanks.

seeking help in a crisis

During the Second World War, Leonard Wilson, then Bishop of Singapore, was captured and tortured by Japanese soldiers. When a tormentor asked him, "Why doesn't God save you?", Wilson replied, "God does save me; not by freeing me from pain, but by giving me the spirit to bear it."

We do not have to undergo what Wilson endured, but from time to time we all have to face a crisis. Sickness can strike suddenly; we may have to come to terms with the death of a relative or friend. Other "crises" may be relatively minor – because sometimes we pour deeper anxieties into trivial setbacks. For example, I may cope well with the news of my father's illness, while overreacting to a car breakdown. Whatever our problems, prayer can help us to deal with them or to put them in perspective.

Having "someone to turn to" is a familiar reassurance in our daily lives. When life gets tough we can always turn to the divine. Stepping back from the situation and presenting it to the divine in prayer may calm us and make us aware that we *can* cope.

If we are deeply shocked, however, we may doubt the existence of the divine or the effectiveness of prayer. Then it is worth making an effort of will to lay our doubts aside and to call on our inner light for help. In the way that a Hindu will repeat a mantra or sacred phrase to sustain awareness of the godhead, try repeating your chosen name for the divine as a stopgap measure until your faith is sufficiently restored to see you through the crisis.

exercise eight

catch the safety line

In a crisis the practice of slowly repeating a sacred word or inspirational phrase has remarkable power to restore us to calm and keep despair, panic and even physical pain at bay. This exercise provides a safety line to grasp when we are too angry or upset to think of anything to say to the divine.

1. *Find an uplifting statement or mantra that has calming and positive resonances for you. Phrases such as "I have loved you with an everlasting love" (Jeremiah 31: 3), "Om Mani Padme Hum" ("Hail the Jewel in the Lotus", a Buddhist mantra of compassion) or "I am life's goal, your home and shelter, your dear, true friend" (words of Krishna in the* Bhagavad Gita) *are ideal. It does not matter whether the words were originally spoken by the divine or by a worshipper, so long as you find them inspiring.*

2. *Take as long as you need to memorize your statement. Let the sound of the words resonate through you and imagine they are filling you with positive energy.*

3. *Now think of each word in your prayer linking to the next to form a safety line that connects you to the divine. As you repeat the words, breathing deeply, the connection becomes stronger and you feel yourself fill with renewed strength and purpose.*

love and adoration

Imagine, if you can, a companion in life who is all things to you: nurturing like a mother, inspirational like a youthful friend, demanding like a stern teacher, reliable like an old colleague, a source of delight and comfort like the perfect husband, wife or partner. The divine power is all these things – and more besides. How would you tell such a perfect partner of your love?

Meera, a tenth-century Indian princess who became a wandering pilgrim, sang a hymn in which she praised the divine (in her case, the Hindu god Krishna) as being her complete fulfilment: her life, joy, beauty, wealth, friend, home, mother, father, guide. Spend a few moments considering what words feel right for you. When you pray try to switch off your analytical mind: follow your inspiration as you speak with the expressive language of love.

Your devotion may be so strong that you are inspired to repeat words of adoration. Some people choose to pray, again and again, "I love you", or to repeat, as if they were the words of God to them, "You are my precious child: I love you." Prayers of love and adoration are prayers of the heart. If such words come naturally to you, let them flow in your dialogue with the divine. As you experience an intimate and strengthening connection with the divine, you may feel acceptance, forgiveness and peace wash over you. It may be sudden, breathtaking, like falling in love at first sight; or it may be gradual. Either way, you recover your natural state – whole, peaceful, fearless and loving.

exercise nine

feel the divine embrace

To awaken ourselves to the divine presence in our hearts is crucial for our sense of joy. Less important is the question of how we choose to address that divine being. This exercise helps you to recall that you are held in a tender embrace by the divine and is designed to encourage you in prayerful adoration.

1. Sit upright in a straight-backed chair. Close your eyes and breathe deeply. Consider the vastness of the universe, the stars beyond number, the rolling expanse of space. Think also for a minute or two of the tiny perfections of the universe — the beauty of a spider's web laden with dew, the intricacy of a snowflake, the dance of electrons around an atomic nucleus.

2. Recollect that the divine power driving the universe is not remote but is intimately connected with you and cares for you minute by minute.

3. Think of the way you might carry or cuddle a child. Picture yourself carried and loved by the divine.

4. Consider the intimate words of devotion you might use to your lover, your child or your friend. Use whatever words feel right to express your delight in the divine embrace. Carry the experience of security and love with you everywhere you go, whatever you do.

51

a union of love

At the start of a new relationship, silences can sometimes be awkward; people usually seek to fill them with chatter. But as our love for the person deepens, we begin to sense a mutual understanding, and can relax into silence. In the most intimate relationships, indeed, people often communicate more express-ively through gesture, touch and simple togetherness than through speech. Your loved one understands your feelings by the way you look, caress and kiss him or her, by the way you understand with-out being told – by the quick intimacy between you.

My beloved is mine and I am his.

SONG OF SOLOMON 2: 16

Our relationship with the divine is the most intimate, secure and loving relationship we have. We cannot touch the divine, but in the intense closeness of our prayer relationship we can in time move beyond speaking and asking to an intimacy like that we sometimes enjoy with our husband, wife or partner in loving quiet and spiritual oneness. The fullest expression of our dialogue with the divine is a union of love and silence.

Mystics will say that their silent, rapturous unity with the divine in prayer and meditation is best described by comparison with the passionate intimacy enjoyed by human lovers. al-Hallaj, a tenth-century Sufi (Muslim mystic), spoke – like the medieval Christian mystic St Teresa of Avila – of being ravished by God, and expressed the act as a moment of spiritual union or identity: "I am He whom I love, and He whom I love is I." According to Indian tra-dition, the god Vishnu, incarnated as the playful cowherd Krishna,

danced with several young married women in a moonlit tryst, and had a romantic affair with one of them, Radha. A magnificent twelfth-century poem, the *Gita Govinda* (*Song of the Cowherd*), by Jayadeva, describes their love. After a disagreement the lovers part and, agonizingly, Radha is left alone; but finally the god returns and they are reconciled. Hindus understand Radha to represent the human spirit in its longing for union with the divine.

Whether we find such imagery compelling or uncomfortable depends to a great extent on our cultural background and our personal propensities. Some may find the idea of union almost blasphemous. Others simply see themselves as belonging to a more disciplined, less expressive tradition of spirituality. Anyone hesitant to imagine the union with the divine as in any way ecstatic may like to think of ecstasy merely as a metaphor: if the best human relationship equates to a hundred, our relationship with the divine equates to infinity.

One word from the world of human relationships that is certainly appropriate, however we may envisage God, is intimacy. And we all know that intimacy cannot be rushed. A deepening of mutual understanding between lovers or close friends can take years of being together and learning about one other. Similarly, in our relationship with the divine it can take a great deal of patient dedication to prayer and sincere inward questing before we truly experience the union of love.

To experience such intimacy we must follow a regular habit of prayer, a form of spiritual cohabitation that brings us to understanding through constancy of contact. I spoke earlier about setting up a prayer line – a means of communication available to us in times of crisis. However, in a shared living space no such special line of communication is necessary: our dialogue with the divine is as natural as breathing, as comprehensive as thinking.

Take one step toward God and God will take a thousand steps toward you.

THE PROPHET MUHAMMAD

Once embarked upon, the intimate dialogue will deepen of its own accord. Indeed, the hardest thing might be to make a start – our first tentative overtures to the divine. Try to open your inner self to divine love by imagining the sense of freedom that comes from stripping away the layers that obscure your true self. Don't be discouraged. It is the testimony of seekers in prayer that all the time we are intently searching for the divine in our devotions, the divine is looking for ways to connect to us.

ONE GOAL, ONE LOVE

The Hindu teacher Sri Ramakrishna (1836–1886) said that he had followed the paths to enlightenment described in all the major religions. He declared that although different traditions used various routes, they all met in the same experience of joyful union with the divine. "God has made religions to suit different aspirants, times and countries," he wrote. "All doctrines are only so many paths." Ramakrishna taught that the worship most pleasing to the divine was our service to others.

exercise ten

melt with love

We cannot produce at will the rapture of adoration felt by Radha for Krishna or by the Sufi mystics for the Beloved. But we can practise settling into relaxed silence. This exercise is designed to help you practise letting your thoughts and concerns go as you dissolve into silence and the presence of the divine.

1. *Read these words written by Manikavacakar, a ninth-century mystic from southern India, in praise of the Hindu god Shiva:*
I will melt like wax in the flame,
Crying out without ceasing,
"My beloved Father".
2. *Imagine yourself dissolving like a candle with love for the divine. Relax: let go of your thoughts; do not try vigorously to banish them, simply detach yourself from them, watch them at play like shadows on the wall of a candlelit room.*
3. *As you feel yourself melting away, give up your fears, resentments and worries, and taste only love – for the divine and for all beings. When you go back to your daily life, look for the divine at play in all things.*

asking for help

Help me

Help me to be one of the righteous ones at all times. Strengthen me to work for the active propagation of righteousness ... that I might prove a worthy worker in the inauguration of your kingdom of righteousness.

Based on an ancient Zoroastrian prayer

Grant us to love you

O Lord, grant us to love you; grant that we may love those that love you; grant that we may do the deeds that win your love. Make the love of you dearer to us than ourselves, than our families, than wealth, and even than cool water.

Attributed to the Prophet Muhammad

Victory

O God, help me to victory over myself, for difficult to conquer is oneself, though when that is conquered, all is conquered.

From ancient Jain scriptures

God's answer

I asked for strength, that I might achieve,
I was made weak, that I might learn humbly
   to obey.
I asked for health, that I might do greater
   things,
I was given infirmity, that I might do
   better things.
I asked for riches, that I might be happy,
I was given poverty, that I might be wise.
I asked for power, that I might have the
   praise of men,
I was given weakness, that I might feel the need
   of God.
I asked for all things, that I might enjoy life,
I was given life, that I might enjoy all things.
I got nothing that I asked for — but everything
   I had hoped for.
Almost despite myself, my unspoken prayers
   were answered.
I am, among all men, most richly blessed.

Attributed to an American Confederate soldier

57

Grant me the ability to be alone

Grant me the ability to be alone;

may it be my custom to go outside each day

among the trees and grasses,

among all growing things,

and there may I be alone,

and enter into prayer

to talk with the one

that I belong to.

Lao Tsu (b.604?BCE), Chinese sage

Help me to feel your presence

O you

who have given me eyes

to see the light

that fills my room,

give me the inward vision

to behold you in this place.

O you, who has made me feel

the morning wind upon my limbs,

help me to feel your presence

as I bow in worship of you.

Chandran Devanesen, 20th-century Indian Christian

Keep me straight

Lord, be the canoe that holds me in the sea of life.
Be the steer that keeps me straight, be the outrigger
that supports me in times of great temptation. Let
your spirit be my sail that carries me through each
day. Keep my body strong, so that I can paddle stead-
fastly on, in the long voyage of life.

New Hebridean prayer

God is the journey and the journey's end

O Father, give my spirit power to climb
to the fountain of all light, and be purified.
Break through the mists of earth, the weight of clay,
Shine forth in splendour, you who are calm weather,
And quiet resting-place for faithful souls.
You carry us, and you go before;
you are the journey, and the journey's end.

Boethius (c.480–524), Roman philosopher

Lead me to light

From the unreal lead me to the real.
From darkness lead me to light.
From death lead me to immortality.

Brihad-Aranyaka Upanishad *(Hindu scripture,
c.10th–5th century BCE)*

Stillness and Silence

Chapter Three

In the hustle and bustle of the twenty-first century, very few of us are accustomed to stillness. Aside from trying out the exercises in this book, when was the last time you sat quietly, without any distractions? Yet learning to sit in silence is fundamental to praying effectively.

When we are still we discover who we truly are, entering our natural state of inner security and peace. Most of the time we are distracted by our likes and dislikes, our physical needs, our worries and plans. But by practising ways to achieve physical and mental calm, we can quieten this inner tumult. It is then that we can see the divine fire burning with an unflickering flame in the depth of our being.

Zen Buddhists say that sitting still, which they call *zazen*, is not only the means to enlightenment but also the end: when you can sit perfectly still, you are perfectly enlightened. On our journey into prayer, too, stillness is both the path we follow and the destination we seek.

meditation and contemplation

Western and Eastern prayer traditions diverge sharply over the practices described by such words as "meditation" and "contemplation". Establishing what writers and teachers from West and East mean by these terms will help us judge the value of different approaches to prayer.

Traditionally in the West, most people have thought of prayer as a way of speaking to God, in whatever form God was imagined. In the East it is more complex. An old story tells that a Christian bishop said to a Buddhist monk, "Isn't it good that we are both people of prayer?" But the monk replied, "I am no one praying to nobody," expressing the Buddhist teaching that there is no permanent self and that the divine cannot be personified.

For Buddhists and Hindus "meditation" is a way of learning to control the mind, which they consider to be like an ox or an elephant – dangerously destructive when wild but very useful when tamed. Christians, on the other hand, have traditionally used the word "meditation" to describe a form of prayer that involves mulling over a verse of scripture or imaginatively entering into a scene described in the Bible. The practice of stilling the mind that is called meditation in the East tends to be known by Christians as "contemplation", and until recently it was mostly reserved for monks and nuns. In this book I have largely used "meditation" in the Eastern sense, with a strong awareness of its usefulness, as both term and practice, in a life of prayer.

There is room in our prayer lives for a wide range of devotional practices, and we should not be afraid to try out different avenues to the inner light. By way of an entrée, try this traditional Christian visualization designed to give you direct imaginative experience of the divine. The exercise uses the story in Mark's Gospel of Jesus calming the storm: "A heavy squall came on and the waves broke over the boat until it was all but swamped. Now [Jesus] was in the stern asleep on a cushion; they roused him and said, 'Master, we are sinking! Do you not care?' He awoke, rebuked the wind, and said to the sea, 'Hush! Be still!' The wind dropped and there was a dead calm." Put the passage away, and

close your eyes to picture Jesus asleep in the boat. Be still and silent for five minutes. Feel the boat rocking in the storm; smell the spray – your clothes are getting wet, you feel scared. At last someone wakes Jesus. He speaks to the storm – and in a moment all is still. The silence after the storm makes you catch your breath. You feel safe, and comforted by the divine's immense power to bring peace.

stilling the body

Imagine trying to speak in whispers to a friend while running along a blustery headland. Gulls come wheeling over and the sea pounds on the rocks below, your blood is thumping in your ears, you are panting from exertion. You and your friend cannot hear each other's whispers. But if you come to a shelter and sit for a few moments, allowing your breathing to slow and your body to relax, you can communicate in quiet voices. Before settling into prayer or any kind of contemplation or meditation, we need to calm the clamour of the body, because if we are distracted in this manner we cannot tune into our inner stillness. There are a number of ways to still the body before prayer.

The most important is to settle into a balanced, comfortable position: this helps you to forget your body and focus on your silent dialogue. The lotus position in yoga – sitting on the floor with spine perfectly erect and each foot on the inner thigh opposite – is often recommended by teachers of meditation because it keeps the body perfectly in balance, enabling us to be still for long periods. But Westerners whose bodies are stiff and unused to yoga find it much easier to sit upright in a straight-backed chair.

Once you have found a comfortable position, try tensing and then relaxing each of your muscles in turn – start with your feet and ankles and work up to your shoulders. Then relax the muscles of your face into a slight smile. Listen to the rhythm of your breathing for a few minutes. Then begin your session of prayer.

exercise eleven

settle into calm

We are almost constantly on the move and bombarded by stimuli during our waking hours. This exercise is designed to remind you of the benefits of spending a few minutes in silence and physical stillness. For now, do not pray or meditate – simply savour removing yourself from the clamour of the world and your incessant activity. Feel yourself relax.

1. *Sit cross-legged on the floor, or if you prefer to use a chair, choose an upright one that will support your back comfortably. Close your eyes and check that your body feels in balance. Ensure that your back is straight; slouching makes it harder to stay alert.*

2. *Visualize yourself sitting in a rowboat on a wide, blue lake beneath a cloudless sky. There is no breeze, no motion on the water. Through the deep, clear water you can see the lake's rocky bottom. You are moored in perfect silence – except for small interruptions made by a leaping fish and a chirruping bird. They are part of nature's music and do not disturb you.*

3. *Feel your body completely still. The stresses and strains of your day cannot touch you here. You can carry this sense of peace with you through the day – from time to time, pause, close your eyes and repeat the visualization for a moment. Try to recapture the calm of this physical stillness before each prayer session.*

65

silencing the mind

Just as the sea remains rough for a while after a storm, so the mind continues to whirr when we withdraw from our busy existence and settle down to pray. In twenty minutes of quiet prayer it may even take nineteen to silence the mind, but that one minute's inner silence is reward enough. Be patient and persevere in seeking to calm your inward mental chatter.

Various practices may help. Stilling the body (see page 64) is an important first step. Some people calm their thoughts by listening to quiet music or a recording of natural sounds, such as waves breaking on the shore; choose a recording that gradually fades away, so that you are delivered into silence. Other people repeat a simple sentence, such as "All shall be well, and all manner of thing shall be well" (a revelation granted to the Christian mystic Julian of Norwich). Do not think about the overall meaning of the words, but repeat them slowly and concentrate on one word at a time.

Try not to worry if your mind wanders. If you catch a thought, let it register and then allow yourself to sink back into pure mind. It may be that you are monitoring your performance and judge that today's silence is not as good as yesterday's. This is a mere distraction: send that thought away. Feelings of repressed anger, frustration or desire may surface from your unconscious. Make a mental note to deal with them later – some people even keep a notepad with them for this purpose. Then let your mind return to its point of focus and again become silent.

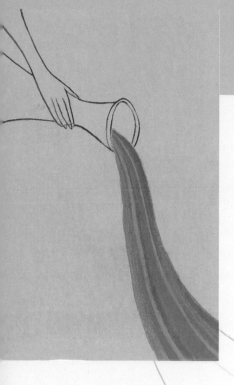

exercise twelve

still your thoughts

Regularly finding a few minutes' mental calm in prayer brings you a sense of perspective on even your most pressing problems. Just as physical stillness (see exercise eleven) gives you refuge from the stresses of daily life, so mental stillness connects you to the calming resources of the spirit. Use this exercise to practise establishing yourself in inner silence.

1. For the next twenty minutes, there is nothing you have to do or think about – no agenda. Breathe deeply.

2. Take the simple phrase "Underneath are the everlasting arms" (Deuteronomy 33: 27).

3. Repeat the words of this phrase slowly. Do not think about what the words mean, but concentrate on their sound. Give your full attention to each word separately, as if they were beads on a string. Try not to picture them as beads, however, as this will distract you.

4. You may feel that you are falling asleep. Sit up a little. Try not to think about how you feel: just concentrate on the words. Enter the silence that grows around you. When you return to the busy surface of consciousness, carry that silence and peace with you into your activities. Feel them flow from you to other people.

prayer and reading

Reading articles, books and excerpts from books that communicate the spiritual experience of others is a good way to develop and refresh your prayer life. A favourite passage from a novel, a line from a poem or a few verses from scripture can offer profound inspiration that draws you back to the writing for years afterward.

Try to vary the types of writing you choose and also the way in which you read them. Reading softly aloud enables you to appreciate the music of the language. A commentary on a piece of sacred writing can offer valuable help by explaining unfamiliar customs or translating language that may be archaic. Try reading a passage, then putting the book aside, closing your eyes and consciously recalling some of the most striking phrases and images.

The scriptures of the world's religions contain a wealth of passages that reward careful and repeated reading. Some people set aside a few minutes for reading sacred texts before prayer, to prepare the mind for communion with the divine. Others report that reading mystical or inspirational writings last thing at night helps ease them prayerfully into sleep. You can find value in scriptures even if you do not believe they are the word of God. Read them as you would a love letter, seeking every ounce of meaning intended by the writer. Bear in mind, too, that many people who use sacred writings in their prayer lives believe that scriptures possess *many* meanings – there is no single correct interpretation.

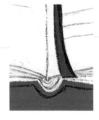

exercise thirteen

uncover the sense

In libraries, in bookstores and on the Internet you have access to an abundance of inspirational writing. Read widely with the aim of enlivening your prayer life. This exercise will encourage you to reflect on your reading. Slowly read through the following poem by a Sufi (Muslim mystic) two or three times and then follow the steps outlined.

> *Before, as was my habit, self I claimed:*
> *True Self I did not see, although I heard it named.*
> *Being self-confined, true Self I did not merit,*
> *Until, leaving self behind, I did Self inherit.*

1. If there are phrases that puzzle you, place a question mark beside them. What possible interpretations of them might there be?

2. If there are phrases that take you by surprise or strike a particularly resonant chord with you, place an exclamation mark beside them. Do they reflect a profound truth with which you identify, or articulate a sentiment you have previously found difficult to express?

3. Now consider the poem's overall meaning. What is the difference between "self" and "Self"? In what ways might you be able to surrender your ego ("self") in order to be united with your true nature ("Self")?

4. Apply the approaches in steps 1, 2 and 3 to other inspirational pieces of writing.

learning to be nothing

The ego often interrupts our concentration, getting in the way of meaningful relationships both with our inner self and with others. Regular prayer can help us guide ourselves by our inner light, to escape the tyranny of the ego. What do you think about when you wash the dishes? If you are thinking about how soon you can get the job done and have a coffee, you are not concentrating on the activity. Whereas if you *are* concentrating, you will have no awareness of your self. You will have become nothing.

The Buddha argued that there is no permanent "I" who experiences life – the ego is a falsehood. He also taught that all existence is characterized by suffering and that the cause of unhappiness is our yearning "attachments" to things, ideas, people; but if we can live with detachment, unhappiness will cease to burden us. It is in this spirit that Buddhists prize meditation, as a means to focus the mind on each moment. This is how we become pure being.

One way to meditate is to empty the mind by concentrating on our breathing. Try sitting still in a quiet place, emptying your mind of thoughts as much as you can, and breathing deeply. Notice your chest rising and falling, and the feel of the air passing in and out of your nostrils. Be aware of how

You are asked to apply mindfulness to your sitting, walking, standing, looking and speaking, and to remain fully conscious in all your activities.

ASHVAGHOSHA
(*c.*100CE),
BUDDHIST
TEACHER AND
POET

70

your sensations change moment by moment. This is meditation. And you can transform meditation into prayer simply by deciding beforehand that each breath you take will be a gift of thanks for the divine presence – and then affirming afterward that you have completed this offering. Alternatively, instead of focusing on your sensations, concentrate on your name for the divine, or on the virtues of someone you are praying for.

Experiment with fusing prayer and meditation in this way. Becoming nothing is not the ultimate self-abasement, the anguished cry that "I am not worthy." It is a tuning in to the divine spirit that dwells in all of us – a glimpse of transcendence.

A CONCENTRATED MIND

I once went with a friend to meet the senior Cambodian Buddhist monk Maha Ghosananda. We had three things to ask him, but he had to leave for the airport in four minutes. His powers of concentration were superb – after he had listened to the questions, he gave such concise answers that there remained one minute in which to discuss mutual friends. As you progress in your prayer life, you may feel the need to develop your concentration: it helps always to do one thing at a time with as much attentiveness as you can manage. A truly prayerful attitude is not nebulously pious: it is highly focused.

learning to be everything

Have you felt a sense of unity with nature – perhaps by a still lake or on a starlit night? As well as helping us to become nothing by moving beyond the ego and living in the moment (see pages 70–71), our prayer lives also nourish within us a deep peace in which we may make our feeling of oneness with the universe a reality that informs our day-to-day living. We can become both nothing and everything.

The sense of unity with nature was described by Richard Jeffries, a nineteenth-century Englishman regarded by his contemporaries as an atheist. He wrote, "I am in it, as the butterfly floats in the light-laden air ... Now is eternity, now is immortal life ... to the soul there is no past and future ... There may be time for the clock ... there is none for me." Jeffries' worship of nature took him beyond self, beyond time, just as a Buddhist monk's mindfulness allows him to escape self and time in an eternal present.

Try this walking meditation, derived from Sufi tradition and designed to cultivate oneness with nature. Take a walk in a favourite park or a place of natural beauty, and imagine that your surroundings are conscious and are watching you pass through them. The trees, the grass, the flowers, the breeze, the birds, the clouds – all have eyes. Gaze back at them, feeling the divine love that sustains the universe pass both ways, from the world to you and from your eyes outward. Feel nature flowing through you, you flowing through nature: this is the divine order of nature in time.

exercise fourteen

find unity with a flower

This exercise in contemplation of a flower will bring you closer to a sense of prayerful unity with the natural world. Try it also with a fruit and a rock.

1. Pick a flower, or find a picture of one that seems particularly beautiful to you. This will be the focus of your meditation.

2. If you wish to devote a defined time to your meditation, set an alarm clock or kitchen timer to go off at the end of it – say twenty minutes later. Or use as much time as you need, stopping when your instinct tells you.

3. Sit in a chair with your back straight and your feet firmly on the ground. Look at the flower through half-closed eyes – try to peer through and beyond it rather than stare at it. Allow the flower's beauty to fill your being. See how the slender stalk supports the head and the petals burst out as if singing for joy.

4. Imagine yourself as the flower – for a few minutes live wholly in the present, like the flower. Imagine energy from the earth rising through your feet and body, as a stem draws in nourishment for the flower. Imagine the muscles in your face "opening" and relaxing as you tilt your head to the sun. When you have finished, or the alarm sounds, return yourself gently to your activities.

discipline as prayer

In the month of Ramadan, Muslims do not eat or drink during the hours of daylight. They refrain as an act of devotion to God and as a discipline to control their bodies. Discipline is not a popular word today, but we need it in our life of prayer. In itself it can be a form of prayer, for when you dedicate an act of self-discipline to the divine, this can be an act of devotion.

We easily become slaves to our appetites or our habits. Small acts of self-denial can transform our frame of mind – and even make us appreciate the things we are giving up. On a weekend or a vacation you could agree with family and friends to give up speaking for a few hours. It might make you ponder whether you

KEEPING A PRAYER JOURNAL

Writing down thoughts and experiences in a journal is a useful discipline that can help us see how we develop in our practice of prayer. Try to make an entry each day: begin by writing a sentence that sums up the day. This might be a comment from the newspaper, something someone has said or a phrase from a scripture. Think about the events of the day. Did anything upsetting happen? Make a note, trying briefly to analyze why you felt angry or hurt. Add a list of events for which you were thankful. Remember that thanksgiving is an important part of prayer and one that reminds us of the essential goodness of life.

sometimes waste your words. If you took the vow, "I will speak the truth" (from the Hindu *Upanishads*), could you keep it? You might discover that your dialogue with the divine becomes more fluent when conducted in silence and inner stillness.

It would be an interesting act of self-discipline to put aside a leisure day on which to do without a few modern conveniences. Why not try giving up television, radio, your CDs, even electric lights for a short spell? Instead, give yourself a few quiet hours of simple acts completed with full concentration. No doubt your inner light will shine all the more brightly on account of this.

When we impose discipline on ourselves – for example, by making ourselves perform worthwhile tasks that we dislike – we are strengthening our resolve and our will. When we come to pray, a stronger will focuses our purpose and helps us to concentrate.

going on retreat

Do you like the idea of a couple of days spent without the telephone, without emails, without even having to make conversation? Many people who are learning to pray find that they benefit from a day or two's retreat from the world in order to develop their inner resources in stillness and silence.

A retreat offers the chance to experiment with contemplative exercises, to read deeply in devotional books, perhaps to enjoy fellowship with like-minded seekers on the path to the divine – in beautiful surroundings or a place hallowed by decades or even centuries of prayer. You can use this as a time of renewal, inspiration and consolidation in your prayer life.

Come away all by yourself to some lonely place and rest for a while.

Jesus,
Mark 6: 31

Some retreats include an artistic activity such as painting, flower-arranging or calligraphy. Others offer talks and meditations led by members of different religious traditions. Retreats do not have to be silent – find out what is intended before you arrive. An organized retreat may be set within a pattern of religious worship, probably with services before breakfast, at noon, in the early evening and just before bedtime. There will be two or three devotional talks; meals will either be in silence or accompanied by someone reading aloud. The rest of the time will be reserved for quiet, contemplation, reading, walking, praying and sleeping. If an organized retreat sounds forbidding, you might prefer to plan your own. Some monasteries, convents and retreat centres offer private retreats, in which you can spend all your time alone.

exercise fifteen

give yourself gifts

Solitary times of prayer may be considered as an unselfish gift from the self to the self. This exercise guides you in planning a spiritually motivated break from the mundane demands of your life.

1. Decide how long you are going to allow yourself on this "treat". A few dedicated hours is enough, but try to give yourself a whole day or even a weekend. Once you have fixed a suitable timeframe, stick to your choice.

2. Where are you going to spend your retreat? If at home, make arrangements to be undisturbed. ensure that housemates or family are going to be away for the duration of your retreat. On the day, unplug the telephone. If your retreat is for a few hours, perhaps spend the time in a local park or a garden summerhouse.

3. What are you going to do on your retreat day? Schedule in periods for prayer and meditation, for rest and for reading. It is a good idea to take several kinds of reading: a devotional text, a work of philosophy, a biography of someone whose life you find inspirational and perhaps some poetry.

4. The day before your retreat spend ten to fifteen minutes in prayer to articulate your aims for your special day (or days). By dedicating your time to specific and well-defined purposes, this final act of preparation will make your retreat all the more fulfilling.

in stillness find inner peace

Stilling the body

I weave a silence on my lips.

I weave a silence into my mind.

I weave a silence within my heart.

I close my ears to distractions.

I close my eyes to attractions.

I close my heart to temptations.

Calm me, O Lord, as you stilled the storm.

Still me, O Lord, keep me from harm.

Let all tumult within me cease.

Enfold me, Lord, in your peace.

David Adam, modern Christian author

God in yourself

Settle yourself in solitude and you will come
upon God in yourself.

Teresa of Avila (1515–1582), Spanish nun and mystic

Waiting on God

In the centre of my heart I have a mystic throne
for you. The candles of my joys are dimly
lighted in the hope of your coming. They will
burn brighter when you appear. Whether you
come or not, I will wait for you until my tears
melt away all material grossness. To please you
my love-perfumed tears will wash your feet of
silence. The altar of my soul will be kept empty.
Until you come I will talk not. I will ask
nothing of you. I will realize that you know the
pangs of my heart while I wait for you. You
know that I am praying. You know that I love
no other. Yet whether you come to me or not, I
will wait for you, though it be for eternity.

*Paramahansa Yogananda (1893–1952), Indian
yoga master*

For quiet hearts

O spirit of God,

set at rest the crowded, hurrying anxious thoughts

within our minds and our hearts.

Let the peace and quiet of your presence take

possession of us.

Help us to rest, to relax, to become open and

receptive to you.

You know our inmost spirits,

the hidden unconscious life within us,

the frustrated desires,

the unresolved tensions and dilemmas.

Cleanse and sweeten the springs of our being,

that freedom, life and love may flow into both our

conscious

and our hidden life.

Lord, we lie open before you,

waiting for your peace, your healing and your word.

George Appleton (1902–1993), English bishop

Peace prayer

Lead me from death to life, from falsehood to truth.

Lead me from despair to hope, from fear to trust.

Lead me from hate to love, from war to peace.

Let peace fill our heart, our world, our universe.

Satish Kumar, modern Jain monk

Perfect peace

You will keep in perfect peace those whose minds

are stayed on you.

Isaiah 26: 3

Be still

Be still and know that I am God.

Psalm 46: 10

The Outward Gesture

Chapter Four

The secularization of the Western world in modern times has pushed traditional religious practices and rituals to the margins of daily life – attending a church or synagogue is often treated as a dutiful social and ethical routine, without spiritual content. However, our relationship with the divine, like all relationships, needs nurturing – and, as a means of expressing our inner commitment, outward gestures become an important part of prayer.

To open a window on the divine, such gestures must be performed with the right attitude. There is no point in carrying out a ritual if we do not invest it with some commitment of belief. Devotion is a reorientation of the self along a spiritual force field. By acting the ritual with sincerity, we place ourselves in a new viewpoint that enlarges our perspective on the divine. Such actions do not need to be grand, public nor traditionally worshipful – doing a painting at home can be enough to build a corridor of prayer.

body language

We all use our hands and bodies when speaking to each other – as you will know if you have been recorded speaking on video as a training exercise. Speaking to the divine is no different. We can choose from a whole repertoire, praying with our bodies and hands, as well as our thoughts and voices.

In some religions, postures are taught as part of the practice of prayer. By standing together in a row facing the holy city of Mecca, Muslims affirm the unity of all believers. Worshippers first express adoration by making a deep bow from the chest, then

---

BODILY PRAYER

Eastern exercise regimes such as t'ai chi and yoga may be used alongside devotional practices as a way of honouring the divine. Hatha yoga, developed in India more than 2,000 years ago and now widely taught in the West as a way to mental and physical health, is in its full sense much more than a physical discipline: its name means union with the divine and the way to union. Yoga works through control of postures and breath to regulate energy flow through centres known as *chakras*, and awaken dormant spiritual powers. The Chinese technique of t'ai chi uses slow, dancelike exercise to control and optimize the body's flow of *chi* or vital energy. When performed with devotion, yoga and t'ai chi can be a form of bodily prayer.

touch knees and forehead to the ground before sitting back on their heels. In other traditions physical expression during worship is spontaneous: at Christian Pentecostal services people may clap, wave their hands and dance in the church aisles.

Using your body in prayer can be eloquently simple, requiring no props. Kneeling is a self-humbling posture that many people find appropriate to their relationship with the One, whereas others might prefer to confine it to particular types of supplication. Although submissive, bear in mind that kneeling is also the posture for receiving ennoblement.

Putting the hands together makes a steeple of flesh – an aspiration to the higher realm. As you pray like this, try fanning your fingers to express the openness of your spirit to God's influence. Or use the contact of fingertips as a focus for meditating on a theme such as separateness and unity – the visible and invisible elements of the cosmos creating a mysterious, harmonious whole.

Supple people might consider learning simple yoga postures in their prayers; especially appropriate is "Salute to the Sun". If you do not know the classic sequence, improvise your own steps to express your acknowledgment of the source of life.

images and icons

For thousands of years artists and craftsmen have drawn inspiration from their piety, making pictures or statues for use as a visual accompaniment to worship. Both looking at and making sacred images can help us as we learn to pray.

A depiction of a god, goddess or holy figure, in many cultures, partakes in some way of the divinity portrayed, and is sacred in itself. However, we do not have to believe in "immanence", as this phenomenon is termed, at a literal level. When we contemplate a sacred image during prayer, we can bring to this act a range of possible attitudes. One approach is to employ the image to focus our mind on one of the special characteristics of the being or figure depicted – perhaps infinite wisdom in the case of a divinity, or charitable self-sacrifice in the case of a saint.

In prayer try focusing on the significant symbolic details such representations often contain – a saint's coarse garments, for example, might suggest a discipline of austerity. With abstract imagery, such as the mandala shown opposite, associate concentric shapes with, for example, the stages of your own spiritual journey.

Artistic quality facilitates prayer by having a subtle impact on the imagination. However, heights of artistic sophistication are not essential: vigorous carvings in the folk tradition can be as meaningful as subtle, realistic modelling. Second-hand imagery, in the form of postcards and art books, is usefully portable – but opt for the highest quality of reproduction you can find, because in the

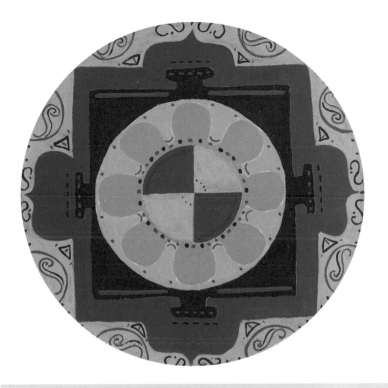

MANDALAS: MAPS OF THE UNIVERSE

Originating in India and prominent in Tibetan Buddhism, mandalas are symbolic pictures of the universe that are used as an aid to meditation. They follow a format. The outer ring is full of flames: as the meditator visualizes entry into the mandala, his or her impurities are burned away. The second circle symbolizes the indestructible quality of enlightenment. A third circle indicates the death of eight superficial mental states that would distract the meditator. A final ring of lotus petals signifies the purity of the realm the meditator now enters. Try making your own mandala and using it in meditative prayer.

colour and detail there is much to stimulate the imagination. Background reading will help you to appreciate details: the Buddha, for example, is sometimes shown with raised hand, forefinger and thumb making a circle in a gesture of *jnana* (teaching).

Sacred art, of course, is often hung in sacred places. Praying before a great religious painting in an atmospheric place of worship often brings about a deep fusion of spiritual and aesthetic responses – appropriate, many would say, because beauty is an outward sign of the divine. There is no reason, however, why you should not pray in front of inspiring art in a gallery: if there are crowds make a virtue of necessity by thinking of the gallery-goers as a procession of fellow mortals on whom the graces of sacred paintings are pouring in profusion, working their subtle influence.

Judaism and Islam hold that physical images of the holy are a dangerous distraction from true worship of the divine, and artists in these traditions have concentrated on abstract imagery and calligraphy or decorative handwriting. If you want to make your own sacred imagery, these forms provide templates that are useful for those with no skill in figurework.

The process is the important thing: the act of making is itself a prayer. Before you start, inwardly dedicate the work as an offering of gratitude and love to the divine, then as you work try to emulate the Hindu craftsmen by letting your mind and spirit work intuitively, suspending your critical judgment. Wait for several hours or a whole day before re-examining what you have produced. Once again say a few words of dedication over the piece.

exercise sixteen

receive divine light

Devotional images have great power to inspire us when we pray. This exercise suggests some ways in which you might relate to an icon, statuette or painting – for example, a picture of Jesus or the Virgin Mary, or a figurine of the Buddha or a Hindu god such as Shiva.

1. Place the image or figure on a table and sit upright in front of it. You might like to light a candle before it. Sit quietly and breathe deeply. Let your mind become still.

2. Contemplate the image or statuette. Open yourself to the spiritual influence of the figure – the selfless love of Jesus, the serenity of the Buddha or the universal energy of Shiva. Most lovers like to look at the beauty of their beloved – focus on the beauty of these qualities.

3. Look particularly at the eyes, which will always have a special concentration of energy. Imagine your inner being opening to the gaze of these eyes.

4. Imagine divine light flowing from these eyes into you, merging with the light of your own inner self. Love, wisdom, fortitude, power, patience – whatever qualities you associate with this image of the divine are within your grasp. You can call on them when you need them.

5. Humbly dedicate yourself to the divine light. Imagine yourself its instrument as you go about your daily life. The light shines in you. Let it flow to others.

flowers and fruit

We make gifts of flowers and fruit to our friends and to those who are ill as symbolic tokens of their presence in our thoughts. In our relationship with the divine, too, offering food or flowers is an expressive way to demonstrate our love. Placing fruits one by one in a bowl can be an apt accompaniment to a prayer of gratitude for abundance or a prayer for the relief of famine. Arranging flowers can be a way to honour the light, to offer beauty back to the divine. When working with flowers in this way, dedicate your time and skills as prayers of gratitude.

Flowers or fruits capture profound truths about time, nature and, by extension, ourselves. The body prospers and fades, but that in itself, in most religions, is no cause for sorrow. Our feelings about such matters tend to be complex – while accepting the truth of our mortality, and the supremacy of the spirit, most of us are emotionally attached to the body. Praying before flowers or fruits can be a way to make an affirmation of faith – that the most important thing in our life is the spiritual awakening inside us, our opening to the divine, not the growth and decay of the physical envelope. At the same time, the beauty of our offering acts as a visible reminder of the inner beauty of an awakened soul.

exercise seventeen

pray through flowers

Flowers, given to us as a gesture of kindness or love, always carry a message. Beyond that sentiment they have rich symbolic associations that make them a suitable focus for prayer.

1. Take a walk in your garden or visit your local florist to select some flowers and leaves for a simple arrangement. Choose three items, to illustrate three stages of life: birth — perhaps a bud; maturity — a fruit or a blossom; decay — perhaps a twig or a small branch stripped of its leaves.

2. At home, feel the texture of the items that you have chosen. Savour their smells.

3. Find a vase and arrange and rearrange your offering until you feel satisfied with the result. Do not follow any rules of composition — simply follow your intuitive sense of whatever looks most pleasing.

4. Think of two or three words or phrases that express your response to your display — perhaps in the manner of a Japanese haiku *(short nature poem). Write them down and dwell upon them.*

5. Sit for a few minutes in silence, with your eyes closed, conjuring up your composition in your mind's eye. Open your eyes, and look at the flowers as if for the first time — feel their profound message enter your spirit. Give a prayer of thanks for the wisdom you have received.

music and song

According to ancient belief, music both honours the gods and has the power to awaken the human heart to the call of the divine. Traditional accounts of heaven often describe vast choirs singing in praise of God. In Hindu myth when the youthful god Krishna summons Radha and other young women to a midnight dalliance that represents the union of the human soul with the divine, he does so by playing haunting melodies on his flute.

Music, both choral and instrumental, plays a large part in communal prayer, uniting people in fellowship and transcending barriers of nationality, colour and religion. In solitary prayer, too, songs of praise have a part to play. Some of the simple, repetitive refrains known as "Taizé chant" (after a Christian community in Taizé, central France) are easy to sing on your own. If you use a mantra for meditation, try singing it to a simple tune. If you play a musical instrument, dedicate your practice sessions to the divine and so make each session an act of prayer.

You may also find listening to music a calming prelude to prayer. It is worth experimenting with music that is unfamiliar to you – perhaps Indian instrumental *ragas*, Tibetan Buddhist chanting, Gregorian or Byzantine Christian plainsong. You could also try listening to sounds of the natural world, such as the songs of whales or the calls of animals and birds in the rainforest (all readily available in commercial recordings). Listening in this way helps to soothe the body and to still the mind.

There are halls in the heavens above that open only to the voice of song.
THE ZOHAR (JEWISH MYSTICAL BOOK)

exercise eighteen

pray through music

Most of us will have a collection of well-loved music recordings that we use to calm ourselves when we are agitated or inspire us when we are dejected. The aim of this exercise is to take advantage of the power of harmony and melody by using music as prayer.

1. Take your time choosing an inspirational piece of music to listen to. Choose something you find uplifting and positive. Do not assume that the music has to be "religious" or quiet and peaceful. Any music that inspires you will serve — opera, soul, folk or reggae may be as useful for your purpose as hymns, Handel's Messiah or medieval plainsong.

2. Choose what you want to pray about and focus on this theme for a few moments. For example, if you wish to pray for an individual's healing, visualize the person.

3. Turn on the music and listen with your full attention. Try not to think about the composer or the performer. Approach your listening as an exercise in concentration and prayerful attention.

4. Now visualize the music as a stream of bright heat energy flowing through you, flooding out to transform the situation or person for whom you are praying. Feel the divine energy in the music, its capacity to bring about positive changes by an invisible outpouring of love.

sacred places

In December 1531, according to tradition, the Virgin Mary appeared to a poor Aztec named Juan Diego on the hill of Tepeyac, now near Mexico City. She instructed him to build a place of worship there and miraculously imprinted on his cloak an image of herself that is still visible today. The first sanctuary was built on Tepeyac in 1533, and almost 470 years later an estimated 10 million Roman Catholics each year visit the basilica that stands there. Sites such as these have a special aura. Any building or landscape feature that has been repeatedly dedicated to the divine by the prayers of visitors will develop an awesome power.

Many sacred places, like Tepeyac, are revered because of their association with a divine figure, a saint or the founder of a faith. Sarnath, in northern India, is reputed to be where the Buddha preached his first sermon and has been a place of pilgrimage for more than 2,000 years. Muslims travel to the holy city of Mecca, in Saudi Arabia, birthplace of the Prophet Muhammad. In some places the sheer grandeur of nature moved our ancestors to declare a site sacred. Mount Fuji, for example, is holy to the Japanese Shinto religion. Aboriginal peoples, especially, have a deep sense of the sacred in nature; in recent years, they have regained possession of a number of ancestral shrines such as Uluru (Ayers Rock) in central Australia.

You may receive powerful inspiration from visiting an established sacred site, whose history you can read and absorb yourself

in. Being in such a place and contemplating its significance, recre-
ating in your imagination its apparently miraculous events, effects
a subtle reorientation of mind and spirit. But you also have the
option of selecting or creating a special place according to your
own inclinations. Try to find somewhere that speaks directly to
your imagination, perhaps a church or temple (ruined or intact), or
a beautiful grove or stream in the countryside: this might become
a sanctuary to which you can retreat when you are stressed or in
need of spiritual renewal.

Equally, you might create a sacred place at home (or even at
work) by dedicating part of your environment to the spirit. A
table, shelf or alcove might be reserved as an "altar" – a place to
house objects that speak to you at a profound level and help you
focus on the divine – perhaps flowers, a candle, or a sacred sym-
bol or picture. Keep the place tidy and fresh-smelling. You might
like to burn incense here. If you pray in this personalized sacred
space, you will find that in due course it becomes associated with
the peace that your relationship with the divine brings you.

Don't be embarrassed by the word "altar", even if initially it
conjures up for you a conservative way of thinking. Possess the
word for your own use (or devise an alternative): imagine its accu-
mulated meanings draining away as you invest the term with your
spiritual identity. When you travel take a few of your treasured
sacred objects with you – a makeshift altar on the move.

pilgrimage

In the Middle Ages Christians travelled as pilgrims to sacred sites to seek forgiveness of their sins, to celebrate the lives and deaths of saints and to recapture their fervour for the divine. For many years the long trip to Jerusalem was the spiritual summit of a Christian's life, but after the Saracens took control of the Holy Land in 1244, Christian pilgrims flocked to destinations closer to home. These included Rome, Canterbury in England (where St Thomas à Becket was killed by knights of King Henry II in 1170), and Santiago de Compostela in Spain (by tradition the burial place of St James, cousin of Jesus Christ).

For any of us a trip to a site associated with a pioneer on the path to the divine can be a moving experience. But remember that the primary purpose of pilgrimage is to refresh our relationship with our inner light, and also that we are free to reinvent the traditional idea of a pilgrimage for our own needs and times. For example, we might decide that our journey will not have a well-documented religious focus: the ruins of an ancient civilization may be just as inspirational as a shrine.

If you can't make a long journey, don't worry – most people have a suitable site within reasonable distance of home (see exercise, opposite). A pilgrimage is an outward symbolic version of the most important prayer journey of all, which we can make without leaving the room in which we are sitting. This is the journey into the depth of our being to discover our true self.

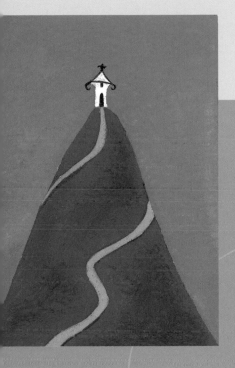

exercise nineteen

take a sacred walk

Some of the medieval Christian pilgrims travelled on horseback and some by carriage, but the traditional way to go on pilgrimage was by foot. This exercise centres on taking a pilgrim's walk in a sacred or inspiring site that is within easy distance of your home.

1. Set aside at least half a day to make a simple pilgrimage. Choose your destination with care – it could be a place of natural beauty or a sacred building.

2. Wear comfortable shoes and take a simple picnic and some water with you (queueing at a crowded cafeteria may spoil the mood). Leave your camera at home. Take a journal, notepad or sketchbook in which to jot down impressions.

3. Make this a restful visit: take your time. Allow yourself some quiet to tune into the site's special atmosphere, and see it as the light changes.

4. Try to feel why the place is special to its guardians. If it is a place of worship, ask if you may attend one of the ceremonies.

5. Allow the atmosphere to work on you, helping you feel at peace with yourself, with other people and with the divine. Think of one insight or resolution to carry back from your pilgrimage to your life at home.

special meals and ceremonies

Many Jewish people, even if they are not strict in their religious observances, keep up the faith's tradition of a Friday evening family meal with prayers to mark the start of the Sabbath or day of rest. They can see the value of a regular time when the family comes together – even if they might not always surround the occasion with any special ceremony.

Throughout history holy days, religious festivals and rites of passage have been marked with special meals. By tradition these meals are not just a sharing with other worshippers but also a symbolic act of communion with the divine. But in secularized societies the celebratory meal associated with a festival often becomes more important than the festival itself, the reason for which may be largely or completely forgotten. Even so, special meals at Christmas, Easter or Thanksgiving – although not overtly times of prayer – help bind a family or group together.

I was once asked to arrange a "cosmic celebration" of the birth of a child by parents who belonged to different faiths. We devised a ceremony to be held in a church, but I now think that it would have been better to integrate the occasion into a meal.

Imagine you are planning a meal to celebrate the birth of your child. You know that your partner and his or her family do not practise any religion and that your friends belong to diverse faiths, but you want to mark your son's or daughter's arrival with a memorable ceremony.

The setting and choice of colours are significant. Flowers, espe-cially in bud, suggest growth. White is associated with purity, yellow with the immortal soul, blue with the cloak of the Virgin Mary. Planning the menu is important, not only for taste, but also for symbolic meaning: eggs, for example, might stand for new life.

Try to include an element of performance. If you have friends who are good singers or instrumentalists, perhaps you can find an appropriate song or piece for them to perform. Can you devise a small ceremony that makes the baby the centre of attention for a few moments, as in a baptism? Guests might be asked to give a reading – there are many wonderful poems about new life. The celebration meal will in this way become a time of blessing.

daily meals

A Hebrew proverb states, "He who eats and drinks without blessing the Lord is a thief." Meals are natural occasions for expressing our gratitude and companionship and, although the custom of saying grace (a prayer of thanks) has largely disappeared, many of us still feel instinctively that a meal requires some ritual. An expression of thanksgiving at the start of a meal binds us together in recognition of life's bounty and gives us a chance to remember all those who have been involved in producing the food.

You do not have buy a book of graces or dredge up half-remembered words from your childhood: experiment with new words and gestures that feel right in your heart and in your home. You might like to lay an extra place at table to remind all present that there are many without enough to eat. Think of a few small rituals that involve everyone. If you have children, before you eat try asking them to say where the food has come from. Perhaps you could ask each person to recount a recent experience, thought-provoking or uplifting – for example, one that has taken place that day.

Graces are not merely for shared dinners. Eating alone can sometimes be rather mechanical: cook, serve, eat – perhaps with the radio or television blaring in the background. But next time you eat alone try pausing in silence before you start: give thanks to the divine for your health and for the food and drink, then imagine yourself offering a portion to the source of life. After this small ritual the meal will nourish your spirit as much as your body.

Each time we eat, may we remember God's love.

CHINESE PRAYER

exercise twenty

before we begin

Try experimenting with simple pre-meal rituals to find one that suits you and the people with whom you eat. This exercise suggests a pattern of ritual to affirm the fellowship of those eating together and to express gratitude for good health and food.

1. When you lay the table place some candles in the centre. Once everyone is settled light the candles. This reminds the people around the table that every shared meal is a special occasion.

2. Ask the people to hold hands and be quiet for a moment. Holding hands emphasizes the act of coming together while the silence allows each person a moment for his or her private reflections.

3. If you wish, say a few words of thanks to the divine for food, companionship and good health. If you would rather not do this, simply ask everyone to join in saying "A blessing on the meal".

4. Now try to carry the concentration you brought to this brief moment of thanksgiving on into the meal. Pay attention to the flavours, textures and colours of the food. Listen attentively to your fellow diners. The meal that you have dedicated to the divine becomes nothing less than a sacred ritual and expression of togetherness.

using a prayer book

Chefs usually know how to prepare a meal without consulting a recipe book, partly because their experience allows them to innovate successfully. But from time to time they do take a look at books of recipes, to stretch their imagination or try something new. We can pray to the divine in any way we like, at any time, in any words. Yet sometimes we will probably find it helpful to read the prayers of others – like a recipe book for a chef, an anthology of prayers can bring us inspiration and fresh perspectives.

There are many published collections, some drawing on numerous religions, some dealing with the most everyday topics in everyday language. A few of the best anthologies are listed in the bibliography of this book – experiment until you find one that speaks to your spirit. In addition, I would recommend that you buy a small, sturdy notebook in which to make your own collection. Note down anything you find inspirational – prayers, poems, lines from songs, sentences from novels, quotations from newspapers, dialogue from films or television, snippets of advice in your friends' letters. Carry the book with you and memorize the prayers and passages that you find most helpful. Then you will have inspirational words available at times of need.

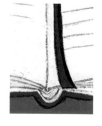

Making a collection absorbs you in the prayers and meditations of many eras, regions and faiths, reminding you that you belong to a great fellowship of people who have prayed – even if you feel that you are an exception among your acquaintances. If your prayer life

has gone dry or you feel isolated from your inner light, reading others' prayers is a helpful way to sustain and perhaps refresh your routine. When you feel inspired to write your own prayers (see exercise, page 107), you can collect them here too.

After praying note down anything that occurs to you about the progress of your prayer life, what insights you have gained, what thoughts occur to you, however random. You will probably find you are at your most creative after sessions of prayer. Indeed, from your jottings at these times new prayers will often take root in an organic process of self-revelation.

prayer and daily life

Just as doctors advise daily exercise, so spiritual guides recommend daily prayer. Muslims are expected to pray five times a day, and almost all traditions suggest a time of prayer in the peace of the early morning, when the world is awakening, and in the evening, as the lamps are lit.

This prayer timetable derives from an agrarian society, and does not allow for shiftwork, commuting and other aspects of modern life. Early morning prayer helps you to start the day in a grounded, peaceful frame of mind, but it may not be possible if you have to care for a sick relative or help young children prepare for school. Prayer in the late evening enables you to wind down for sleep in the presence of the divine, but, again, family or work commitments may make this impossible. Yet the advice to pray regularly is based on a sound principle – that a routine is invaluable if you are to make progress in prayer.

The right time to set aside for private prayer is any time when you can regularly be sure of being uninterrupted. This may take some effort and ingenuity: have a look at your daily timetable and draw up a short list of activities – even seemingly worthy ones – that are not truly productive. The adventure of learning to pray is

worth any number of small sacrifices. Once you have established a pattern, you will find that you feel spiritually unkempt if you miss a session – just as you feel physically scruffy if you leave for work without washing your face or brushing your hair.

In reshaping your routine in this way to make space for prayer, be sure not to fall into the trap of making a hermetic seal between prayer time and "real" time. Quite apart from your regular periods of solitary communion with the divine, remember to carry prayer with you as you go about your daily life. When St Paul told the Christians at Thessalonica to "pray without ceasing", he did not

Rejoice evermore. Pray without ceasing. In everything give thanks.

ST PAUL,
*1 THESSALONIANS
3: 17*

MINDFUL EXERCISE

There is a Buddhist practice known as "walking meditation" in which you concentrate your mind on the act of walking – being conscious of every movement and of the feel of the ground as your foot touches the ground. Such concentration encourages total attention on the present moment. Of course you can adapt walking meditation to swimming, gentle running or dancing. The latter we all know can be a great release when we are stressed. Try dedicating your dancing to the divine: feel your tension fly from your hands and feet. Joy rises in you as you dance. Try to banish self-consciousness and concentrate fully on the moment, on your movement to the music.

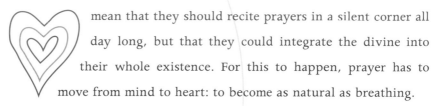

mean that they should recite prayers in a silent corner all day long, but that they could integrate the divine into their whole existence. For this to happen, prayer has to move from mind to heart: to become as natural as breathing.

In the mid-nineteenth century a Russian pilgrim who asked a hermit how to obey Paul's words was taught the "Jesus prayer". It is simple to describe, if not to practise: you begin by saying over and over again with your lips, in time with the rhythm of your breathing, "Lord Jesus Christ, have mercy on me", or a similar phrase. When you have lived with the prayer long enough, the words move to your mind, rather like a catchy tune, and from there they move to your heart and become as natural as your heartbeat. If you like the idea of reciting a mantra, this can have a similar effect – the sacred phrase you have chosen reverberating in the core of your being. Bringing this about may take years, and the effect cannot be forced, but when it does occur you will live your entire life in the presence of the divine.

Try repeating the Jesus prayer or a mantra as you walk. The motion of your body makes your breathing rhythmic, so that the prayer is more likely to permeate your inner self. You can do this too with any physical exercise that does not require careful concentration – such as jogging or swimming. After your next morning prayer session, choose one short, simple activity in the day ahead – perhaps a few minutes' tending the garden, doing a little housework, cooking the evening meal – that you will attempt to do prayerfully. Your life will be enriched.

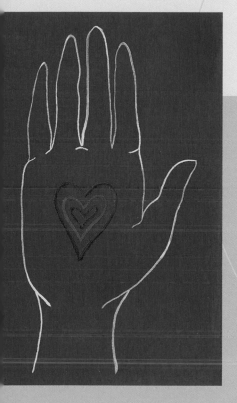

exercise twenty-one

write a morning prayer

This exercise is designed to help you write a prayer for making an intimate connection with the divine each morning. It does not matter if you feel a little uncomfortable at first when expressing yourself on paper this prayer is for your own use, not for other people.

1. Equip yourself to write your prayer by finding a pencil and two pieces of paper.

2. Consider how you want to address the divine – for example, Lord, Beloved, Friend, Father, Mother, Teacher, Self. Now, eyes closed, try to visualize the divine – perhaps as a ball of light or a blazing tree.

3. Think of yourself in the morning. What are your routines? Then think about the course of the day. What are its greatest challenges? What are you grateful for each day? Open your eyes and jot down your thoughts.

4. Take the other piece of paper and write out your prayer. Begin by addressing the divine in your chosen form and offering a prayer of thanks for the new day. Then write a sentence for each of your notes about your daily activities – perhaps asking for calm and love in organizing yourself and your family before you leave the house, clarity or creativity in your work and so on. Finish by asking for a safe return home in the evening.

5. Finally, make a promise to yourself to spend ten quiet minutes each morning with your prayer.

the rhythm of life

Meet God and stand by him

God is ... where the tiller is tilling the hard
ground and where the pathmaker is breaking
stones ... meet God and stand by him in the toil
and sweat of your brow.

Rabindranath Tagore (1861–1941), Indian writer

My heart, beating with joy

My heart, beating with joy
fills the tall air beneath the forest trees with song,
fills the forest, my home, my mother, with singing.
I have captured a tiny songbird in my net –
a tiny bird,
and my own singing heart
is caught with that bird in my net.

Adapted from a pregnancy song of the Efé peoples

Blessing of a new house

May the inhabitants of this dwelling place be
blessed with many children, may they enjoy
wealth, may they be generous to the poor; may
they escape disease and trouble, may they be
safe these many years.

Adapted from a prayer of the Nyola, Kenya

Harmony with the divine

As a conductor and musicians are part of one
orchestra, as limbs and muscles, sinews and
blood part of one body, help us to see that each
of us is important to creation as a whole; that
your rhythms and your tempos are music to our
lives as long as we keep in harmony with you,
now and through all eternity.

Giles Harcourt, modern Christian author

Sacred Earth

Teach your children what we have taught our
children, that the Earth is our Mother.
Whatever befalls the Earth, befalls the children
of the Earth.
God is the God of all people ...
and what is humankind without the beasts? ...
all things are connected. This we know,
the Earth does not belong to humans,
humans belong to the Earth.
This we know,
all things are connected like the blood which
unites one family.
All things are connected.

*Words of Chief Sealth of the Native North American
Suquamish, c.1855*

You open wide your hand

The eyes of all look to you in hope
and you give them their food in due season.
You open wide your hand
and fill all things living with your bounteous gift.

Psalm 145: 15–16

Four prayers from China

When opening a door:
I pray you, Lord, to open the door of my heart
to receive you within my heart.

When washing clothes:
I pray you, Lord, to wash my heart and make
me white as snow.

On building a wall:
I pray you, Lord, to make my faith as firm as a
house built on a rock.

On sowing seed:
I pray you, Lord, to sow the seed of virtue in
my heart.

*Prayers written in the 1930s for the Christian
Homes movement in China*

An all-embracing love

Love all God's creation – the whole of it ...
Love every leaf, every ray of light. Love the
animals, love the plants, love everything. If you
love everything, you will perceive the mystery
of God in all ... you will come at last to love the
whole world with an all-embracing love.

Fyodr Dostoevsky (1821–1881), Russian novelist

Self and Others

Chapter Five

According to the English philosopher A.N. Whitehead (1861–1947), religion is "what the individual does with his own solitariness". But prayer can be a communal as well as a private activity: it strengthens the bonds of a community by encouraging tolerance and forgiveness; and it provides a framework for the expression of mutual support.

Traditional communities were usually built around a single belief system, making harmony through prayer an almost automatic phenomenon. In the modern world, where people of diverse cultures live in the same space, a flexible and creative approach to prayer and communal ritual can build bridges and be a powerful tool for unity and peace.

Even in solitude, of course, prayer is not focused solely on ourselves: we are moved to pray for those we know who are sick or who have been bereaved, or perhaps for a suffering group such as refugees or earthquake victims. One of the most enriching uses of prayer is to seek help for others.

private prayer, loving service

To the twenty-first century's individualistic vision, private prayer may seem like another chance to focus on the purely personal, an essentially solitary, highly charged adventure in search of the inner light. But praying alone unites us with other people and other forms of life: the more we encounter the divine in ourselves and see it in others, the closer we come to understanding that others' distress is ours also, and the more we want to act in compassionate service. As we understand and feel the sacredness of life, we are drawn to live in harmony with others.

Prayer leads us to interaction with others, persuades us, if we think about it, that private devotions are the centre of a network of spiritual influence. With the help of prayer, we contribute more effectively in society. Imagine yourself in prayer breathing in the peace, strength and compassion of the divine. Now see yourself in your workplace or helping someone in trouble, breathing out into others' lives the strength you took in during prayer.

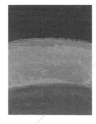

"Know thyself": the imperative inscribed on the Ancient Greek Temple of Apollo at Delphi is of pressing relevance for us as we learn to pray. Through private prayer we can come to self-awareness and self-acceptance, solid and necessary foundations for interaction with others. In prayer we can develop the qualities of patience and loving kindness that we need in the challenging situations we will encounter during the day. If we are at peace, we can spread peace.

exercise twenty-two

marginalize yourself

The feeling that each of us is unique and isolated, as individuals, can lead us into spiritual pitfalls. Our apparent inability to reach out to others formed the basis of the philosophical movement known as Existentialism. In fact, however, prayer enables us to bridge the Existentialist chasm. This exercise is a spiritual workout that breaks down our isolation.

1. Sit quietly and comfortably, close your eyes, and picture yourself walking into a beautiful sunset.

2. Imagine a disembodied voice – a kind of devil's advocate – saying to you that the sun was made for your benefit alone. Rehearse to yourself any arguments you might raise to refute this proposition.

3. Imagine yourself surrounded by people, ranged in concentric circles around you. Your family and close friends are in the innermost circle, nearest to you, your work colleagues in the second circle, strangers you have encountered in an outer circle beyond that, and so on. Populate your mental picture until it becomes dense with transactions and encounters.

4. Choose, at random, someone in one of the outermost circles of your pattern, and imagine the pattern that he or she has created. You are there somewhere – if he or she remembers you – but only as a minor figure. Pray for others, from this other person's perspective.

sharing prayer

Praying with others brings a sense of fellowship, and strength through togetherness. Learning to pray is a challenge and, when you are doing something challenging, it can help to work with others – it is easier, for example, to train for a half-marathon in a group than on your own because group support helps you carry out your good intentions. As you learn to pray, why not turn to a worshipping community for friendship and guidance?

It is sweet to have friends in need, and to share prayer is sweet.

DHAMMAPADA (BUDDHIST SCRIPTURE)

Visit some of the churches, temples, mosques or synagogues in your area. You might consider reestablishing links with your family's tradition, or instead choose to investigate a new community. Perhaps you have friends who attend a church or temple. Why not ask if you might go with them one day? It is worth taking time to find out a little more about it before you make the visit. Most places of worship welcome visitors, but there is no harm in making a telephone call to check with a minister or official which is the most appropriate service or meeting to attend, and whether there are special requirements for visitors. For example, at some Jain temples you are not allowed to wear anything made of leather, and at a Sikh *Gurdwara* you will be asked to take off your shoes and to cover your head. Usually you will receive a very warm welcome.

THE WATER CEREMONY

The unity generated by communal prayer within a particular religious tradition is usually positive but often narrow in its focus. New rituals such as the Water Ceremony, first used at the launch of the Year of Interreligious Understanding and Co-operation in 1993, celebrate values shared by members of different traditions of faith. Representatives of each religion bring a gift of water and pour it into a fountain, saying together a carefully chosen nondenominational prayer that dedicates the ritual to the end of conflict and the renewal of hope. You can try creating your own water ceremony for use on significant occasions such as birthdays in a multi-faith prayer group.

If you feel drawn to take part in communal prayer but have not been to a place of worship for a long time, it might be easiest to start by going to a small group meeting. A wide range of small groups attached to churches, temples and synagogues meet for meditation and prayer, often in people's homes where the atmosphere is generally warm and friendly. Feel free to experiment – and persist until you find the fellowship that is right for you and encourages you in your exploration of prayer.

You might decide to take the plunge and set up your own fellowship group for prayer. Try inviting a few friends to your home to discuss the idea of the group; if they are doubtful about coming, tell them they will be welcome whatever their beliefs and whether or not they pray regularly. You will need to prepare a room in your home – provide enough space for the group members to sit in a circle or semi-circle; the chairs should be of much the same height. When everyone is settled introduce your plan and let other people comment; after some discussion try a short time of prayer together. Begin by playing a little quiet music and invite people to be silent for a few minutes. Read three prayers you have found helpful. Give others a chance to read their favourite prayers. End, perhaps, with the words, "Peace to all of you", or something similar. If your friends are of different faiths, encourage them, if you continue with these gatherings, to share a little about how they were taught to pray – this will broaden everyone's idea of prayer.

Communal prayer can be a source of strength, but it is not a requirement of learning to pray. Don't worry if, for any reason at all, the idea of group prayers is either unappealing or impracticable for you. Some people simply do not feel comfortable praying with others. You are part of a vast network of people praying, whether or not you are bodily with them. Like a spider's web this prayer network is wonderfully strong, even if its strength seems to defy the assumptions of common sense. Remember, once again, to pray as you can, not as you can't. You have a direct relationship with the divine in the core of your being – and this intimate relationship is unchanging whether you are shipwrecked on a desert island or living in the heart of a bustling city.

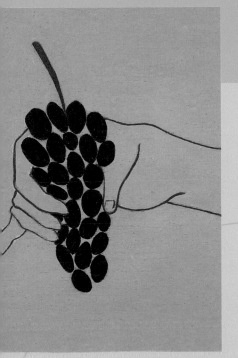

exercise twenty-three

make a gathering

Any gathering for thanksgiving, blessing or supplication is a positive event whose energies will spread
among all participants and create a bond of fellowship.
Faith can make an impact on the world – and any
group of people gathered for prayer is a microcosm of
the more caring, spiritual society for which many of us
hope and pray. Here are some suggestions for planning
a special gathering to commemorate a season or birth-
day, a partnership or project, or to pray together for
personal or social healing.

1. *Choose a suitable place. In summer an outside
location might be appropriate, especially if the occasion
is a happy one. But check that extraneous noise will not
make it too difficult for people to hear each other.*

2. *Draw up the guest list. Two key decisions need to
be made: Will children be invited? (They add vitality but
might not adapt well to the mood of a solemn occasion.)
And will strangers, or acquaintances, be asked to come?
(If so, you might wish to visit them privately beforehand
to discuss what is involved.)*

3. *Script and choreograph the gathering. One possible structure is a keynote prayer framed by suitable
readings or music, or perhaps a dance. The more people
participate, with their special talents, the stronger the
bonds that will be cemented by the gathering.*

119

celebration and custom

I n seeking a yearly cycle to acknowledge in our life of prayer – a series of public milestones at which to pause, rest awhile and pray appropriately – we need look no further than the calendars by which major religions, past and present, have organized their communal festivals.

Today in the West secularization means that any link between time off work and religion – other than sun worship! – is largely dissolved. Yet it is rewarding to renew the original meaning of a holiday, or "holy day". Invigorate your prayer life by borrowing some of the devotional words specially written for, say, a Christian saint's day or an Islamic or Hindu festival.

It is rewarding, too, to mark the turning points of the agrarian year – the solstices and equinoxes, the times of sowing and harvest. The Celts were particularly close to the cycles of the land, and they devised great rituals – the fire ceremonies of Samhain (end October/early November) and Beltane (May Day), the times of milking (Imbolc, early February) and of harvest (Lughnasa, 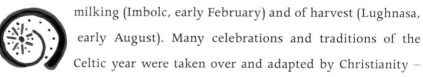 early August). Many celebrations and traditions of the Celtic year were taken over and adapted by Christianity – for example, spirits on the rampage at Hallowe'en. Delve into the mysteries of ancient ceremonies, and see if you can produce new versions of them in your prayer life.

Rituals and customs preserve shared memories and common values. Many people, however, have lost touch with the symbolic

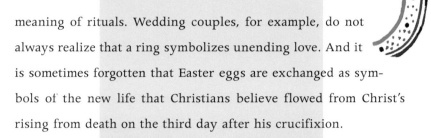

meaning of rituals. Wedding couples, for example, do not always realize that a ring symbolizes unending love. And it is sometimes forgotten that Easter eggs are exchanged as symbols of the new life that Christians believe flowed from Christ's rising from death on the third day after his crucifixion.

Investigate how your family traditionally celebrated festivals. Ask your grandparents or others of their generation how they acknowledged special times of the year as children, and what they understood different customs to mean. If you have children of your own, encourage them to ask these questions and to write down their findings in a journal. You could also ask the older generation to write down their memories. Such a process of transmission strengthens family identity, and might well – by reviving the memory of traditional religious habits – lead to a renewed sense of the sacred. The resulting book would be a family heirloom.

One reason why traditional rituals are being forgotten is that patterns of life are changing. For example, marriages between partners of different cultures, or celebrations of long-term relationships between people who choose not to marry or between gay or lesbian partners, require specially created rituals. All you need is imagination, and a willingness to adapt existing prayers to new situations – or to write your own, new prayers. As societies mingle and the boundaries of acceptable behaviour change shape, our prayer life needs to keep up with the times.

seeking forgiveness

The Hindu saint Ramalingam (1823–1874) spoke of the divine as a protective Mother and Father "dancing in mercy in the hearts of all lives". We all fail to live up to the standards of behaviour we set ourselves, and sometimes may feel painfully aware of this, but in prayer we can discover forgiveness.

The Greek word translated as "sin" was originally a term used in archery for missing the mark. Rather than making us feel guilty and unworthy, recognition of our wrongdoing should encourage us to live better lives. If we have hurt another person, we need to apologize and if possible to make amends. Sometimes we still feel a weight on our conscience – then it may be helpful to talk the matter over with a friend or spiritual guide. Alternatively you may find the exercise (opposite) helpful. The exercise might at first remind you of the branch of Japanese Buddhism in which to gain entry to Paradise we have only to speak its name; but it is designed to be performed only after you have made reparation for your faults, vowed not to repeat them, yet still find yourself burdened by guilt. To reassure ourselves that we are truly sorry, we might like to undergo a form of penitence and absolution – so that we can move on instead of being held back by a sense of our unworthiness.

LAY DOWN YOUR MISTAKES

If you feel ground down by a sense of having done wrong, you may find it helpful to visualize yourself carrying your mistakes into the divine presence. Imagine that you have been climbing a steep slope, lugging your mistakes in a sack on your back. You come upon a clear pool; lay down the sack and bathe in the deep water. When you emerge, refreshed, the sack has been removed. You lay a flower by the pool as an offering of thanks.

The first step to gaining forgiveness is self examination. This can be usefully integrated into your regular routine of prayer. Before each prayer session review the commitments you made in the previous one, and examine your behaviour in the interim. After itemizing any ways in which you have fallen short of your commitments, and any selfish acts that might have caused others distress, put your shortfallings in the embrace of the divine with a firm and heartfelt affirmation, such as: "Today I leave my mistakes here and make a new beginning." Bow your head and feel the accepting balm of the divine course through you.

Learning to forgive ourselves is deeply empowering – not least because it helps us to forgive others. However, if your find yourself needing forgiveness over and over again during a short period, perhaps you need seriously to rethink the way you are living?

forgiving others

Saying sorry to ourselves and to the divine is hard enough, but to forgive another person who has hurt us can be even more difficult. Yet in prayer we can find the strength to do this.

Although to forgive is not the same as to forget, a key to forgiving is being able to let go of the past. We are all tempted at times to dwell on others' behaviour toward us, yet when we give way to that temptation our resentments become great burdens. Instead of struggling to carry them, we should put them down.

Where there is forgiveness, there is God Himself.

ADI GRANTH
(SIKH SCRIPTURE)

Imagine that someone has done us a deeply damaging wrong: say a stranger has caused an accident that injured a loved one. All our thoughts might be filled with the demand for some kind of justice. Even in such a very difficult case, we must try to let go of our anger against the perpetrator. When someone hurts us and we hurt him or her back, we have been drawn into a cycle of violence; forgiving is a powerful act of generosity that breaks the cycle. In the American Civil War, Abraham Lincoln forgave and released a captured opponent. When his captains protested that his soldierly duty was to destroy the enemy, Lincoln declared, "I *have* destroyed an enemy soldier: I have turned him into a friend."

Of course, forgiving is not easy, but empathy and compassion help. By fostering these qualities in us, prayer empowers us to walk away from the resentments that burden us and to forgive those who have offended or hurt us. Use the exercise opposite to make a fresh start to a damaged relationship.

exercise twenty-four

shake hands in prayer

The Dalai Lama, who fled his homeland of Tibet in 1959 following a revolt against Chinese rule there and has witnessed his people's prolonged suffering, has said that we should be grateful to our enemies because they help us to develop compassion. This exercise is designed to enable you to find reconciliation with someone who has offended you.

1. Think of the person — say, a male friend — who has upset you. Reflect on his problems and feelings. Picture yourself in your friend's position and imagine what he is now thinking about you.

2. Consider the following questions. Does your anger do you any good? Does it tell you anything about yourself? Are you angry because you are trying to suppress the feelings that your friend has expressed?

3. Create a scene in your mind's eye in which the two of you stand facing each other. Without speaking, you move forward, smiling and offering to shake your friend's hand. Your friend, smiling back, takes your hand and shakes it warmly. You begin to talk.

4. You are not in competition with your friend for happiness — you want the best for him as well as for yourself. Let go of your resentment. Ask the divine to shower your friend with the gifts of happiness and ful-filment. Finally, pray for his well-being and your own.

empathy in prayer

You are praying for a friend, a young mother who has been told that she may have a terminal illness. You try to identify imaginatively with her and can feel her distress, torn as she is between fear of the illness and concern for her children. Your identification gives great intensity to your prayers and you feel you would do anything you could to help her.

Brotherhood is prayer.

WILLIAM BLAKE
(1757–1827)

Praying with empathy encourages you to think of practical ways to help – by putting yourself in your friend's shoes, you better understand the daily stresses of her life and are able to offer assistance that allows her to devote more energy to recuperating and less to worrying. You offer to collect her children from school, perhaps, or to take them on an outing.

Empathy also adds force to our prayers when we are praying for people we do not know. If you feel moved to pray for the victims of a great injustice or a natural disaster, a leap of imagination in which you identify with their fear and helplessness brings their problems to life for you, stoking a fervour in you to work for change, and perhaps enabling you to see small-scale, achievable ways in which you can contribute toward relieving their plight.

The divine cares for the world through us. The act of petitioning in prayer will often turn itself into a question: "What can *I* do to help?" The Spanish Carmelite St Teresa of Avila told her nuns that the divine had to work through their offices – for there are no hands on Earth but human hands.

exercise twenty-five

offer your support

Praying with empathy requires attentive concentration as we use our imaginative faculties to "tune in" to the needs of others. This exercise is designed to help you practise empathy in prayer.

1. Think of a friend who is going through a difficult time – perhaps his or her long-term relationship has just fallen apart; perhaps his or her home or car has been repossessed because of debt.

2. How is your friend different from you? Would he or she want the same things in this situation as you would? Make a few notes about what you think the differences would be.

3. Write a letter to your friend. If you can, think of three or four positive things to say. Make one or two specific offers of help. Do not send the letter.

4. Now imagine that you are your friend and write a reply to this letter. Your friend responds to your offers of help, pointing out any practical difficulties. In this way you deepen your understanding.

5. Use this exchange of unsent letters as the basis for a prayer for your friend. Concentrate on addressing both emotional and practical needs.

6. As soon as you can, call your friend to offer comfort and support. You may find that some of your prayers have already been answered.

127

intercession and healing

All through life we thrive on encouragement and support. If someone we know is sick or in chronic pain, our empathy and prayers – even at a distance – can make a profound difference.

Of course, prayer is more than simply a mark of support; it is also a transformation. It does not receive much publicity, but there is a body of statistical evidence that praying for the sick does indeed make them better. One study carried out in the late 1980s in the coronary-care unit at San Francisco General Hospital showed that patients who were being prayed for fared better than those from the same unit who were not being prayed for. Some might dismiss such results as the "placebo effect" – whereby the health of

The Lord is the strength of the weak.

ADI GRANTH
(SIKH SCRIPTURE)

PRAYING FOR THE DYING

Prayer is normally for recovery but it may be for a change in attitude from resentment to acceptance. You might pray that a dying person will be reconciled with a relative or that he or she will be conscious of the divine's presence. Prayer should be realistic. If someone is dying it is appropriate to ask that he or she may suffer as little pain as possible. It is more helpful to prepare the person who is terminally ill, and relatives, for death than to connive at a pretence that recovery is likely – such pretence can add to the dying person's loneliness, as there is then no opportunity for him or her to share fears of the unknown.

some patients improved because they believed in the power of prayer to help them. But this does not explain other cases in which patients did not know that people were praying for them, nor laboratory studies showing that prayer can have a marked therapeutic effect even on animals.

Our mental, physical and spiritual selves are more closely connected than we generally believe. Extraordinary energies radiate from people found to have special powers of healing. In praying for the sick, touch them if you can, because touch is a conduit for our gift of love, and for the mysterious energies at our disposal. Prayer can reawaken them to the divine's continuing love: an invalid readily begins to doubt his or her self-worth. At times, though, it might be better to pray silently (certainly if a spoken prayer risks alarming the sufferer, by reminding him or her of last rites).

If you are unable to touch the sick, this does not mean your prayers will be less effective. Trust in the invisible network of healing energies. Prayer may be the last resort of the desperate, but when we pray for someone to be healed we should not see this as an alternative to medicine, nor assume the only answer is physical recovery. Healing is a term that includes spiritual well-being.

facing bereavement

We cannot avoid death. Buddhists tell of a woman whose son had died and who asked the Buddha for medicine for him. The Buddha told the mother to go to the city and visit every house, and when she found a house where no one had ever died, to ask for mustard seeds. Eventually she returned to the Buddha without any seeds. The Buddha said to her, "You are not the only one death has overtaken. This is a common law for all people."

Death – even of an elderly parent or grandparent at the end of a long, rich life – comes as a heavy blow to those left behind. We might be overcome by shock. In quiet reflection we should be honest with ourselves and acknowledge our feelings. Speak openly in

SUPPORTING OTHERS THROUGH LOSS

If friends have to cope with bereavement, hold them in the light of your care. Pray that acceptance will rise within them. As you pray, picture yourself filling with the light of divine love. Imagine meeting your friends in a quiet room. You embrace and the light you carry floods over and through them. Pray that your friends will feel able to celebrate the life that has ended. The best practical help you can offer may well be to listen. Let your friends talk about their feelings for as long as they wish. Listen as attentively and compassionately as you can. Speak openly to them, avoiding platitudes of consolation.

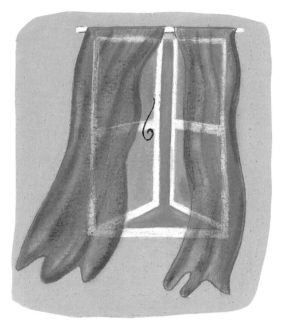

prayer of your grief, of your anger, perhaps of your guilt at having survived or at not having done more for the person you mourn. Ask for the resources to cope with the feelings that flood so powerfully through you.

Take time to share your recollections of the person who has died with friends or relatives, looking back to happy memories of the departed individual when he or she was most alive and fulfilled. This is a time to say "thank you" for joyful times together, and perhaps also to say "sorry". In bereavement many find communal prayer a support. It is also a time when the prayers, poems or other writings of people who have been through the distress of losing a loved one can be profoundly helpful.

Your prayer life may have convinced you that the higher self is distinct from the body and will not cease when the body dies. But whatever our beliefs about life after death, in bereavement we need to find the strength to say goodbye. Imagine your loved one in a ship: as he or she departs this life, you stand on the shore waving farewell, watching the mast dwindle to a point on the wide water. You know that beyond your own horizon is another shore where your loved one will find landfall and a welcome.

teaching children to pray

We worry endlessly about children's physical safety, health and schooling but tend to neglect their development as spiritual beings. Where religious education is provided in schools, it still often focuses on the stories of a particular faith and on learning traditional prayers by heart, rather than on helping children to discover the divine for themselves and learn to pray in a way that suits them.

Encouraging children in a sense of wonder at the universe is an important first step in teaching them to pray. Invite them to smell flowers or quietly to watch birds and insects with you. Take them for country walks (see exercise, opposite). Try to explain these words from a Sikh prayer: "God is in the water, God is in the dry land, God is in the heart."

Teaching the young to evaluate their own and others' experiences helps them to appreciate the world and to be thankful for what is good. You could ask them questions such as: What was the best thing that happened to you today? Why? Was anyone sad? Why do you think they were upset? Lead them in joining hands and saying "thank you" for the special thing that happened and in sending an imaginary hug to the children they felt were sad.

Like adults, children can benefit from learning to sit in silence. Lead children in a period of quiet: make weaving actions as you go through the following prayer: "I weave a silence on my lips; I weave a silence into my mind; I weave a silence within my heart."

exercise twenty-six

respect our planet

An environmental holy day designed to encourage reverence for the Earth may appeal to children and spark an interest in the divine. If possible, invite children from different religious traditions.

1. *Choose a place where the children can wander safely and where you are allowed to have picnics. Before you go, prepare a prayer about trees, leaves and nature. Include a few words about our duty to protect the Earth. Try to make the prayer interactive – perhaps with hand actions or a chorus with which the children can join in. Take food and drink and some picnic rugs.*

2. *When you arrive at the venue, ask the children to search for leaves – encourage them to look for as many different kinds and colours as they can. Give them ten minutes to run around under your supervision.*

3. *Once the ten minutes are up, ask the children to sit down on the rugs and to spread out in front of them the leaves they have collected. Ask them the following questions. Where do the leaves come from? What are the leaves for? Who made the trees?*

4. *Finally, read out your prayer, encouraging the children in the hand movements and chorus. Afterward, celebrate together by eating your picnic. Ask the children to pick up any litter themselves – in small but practical ways they can be custodians of the Earth.*

compassion, forgiveness, peace

Your eyes of compassion

Grant us to look with your eyes of compassion,

O merciful God, at the long travail of humankind:

the wars, the hungry millions,

the countless refugees, the natural disasters,

the cruel and needless deaths,

our inhumanity to one another,

the heartbreak and hopelessness of so many lives.

Hasten the coming of the messianic age

when the nations shall be at peace,

and all shall live free from fear and free from want,

and there shall be no more pain or tears,

in the security of your will,

and the assurance of your love.

George Appleton (1902–1993), English bishop

For my sake

If any differences arise among you behold me
standing before your face, and overlook the faults
of one another for my sake.

Baha'u'llah (1817–1892), founder of the Baha'i Faith

An instrument of peace

Lord, make me an instrument of your peace.

Where there is hatred, let me sow love.

Where there is injury, pardon.

Where there is doubt, faith.

Where there is despair, hope.

Where there is darkness, light.

Where there is sadness, joy.

O Divine Master, grant that I may not so much seek

to be consoled as to console;

to be understood as to understand;

to be loved as to love;

for it is in giving that we receive,

it is in pardoning that we are pardoned,

and it is in dying that we are born to eternal life.

Attributed to St Francis of Assisi (1181/2–1226)

Forgiveness

Father make us merciful as you are merciful
Father of all forgiveness make us forgiving as
you have forgiven us.
Knowing that, with what measure we mete, it
shall be measured to us again.

Eric Milner-White (1884–1963), former Dean of York

Mother of the universe

O Mother of the universe, there is nothing to be
wondered at if you should be full of compassion
for me, for a mother does not forsake her son,
even if he has innumerable faults.
There is not such a sinner like me, neither such
a destroyer of sins as you. O Mahadevi (or great
God), having known all this, do as you think fit.

Sri Shankaracharya (686–718CE), Indian philosopher

The great ship of compassion

O perfect master, you shine on all things and all
people, as gleaming moonlight plays upon a
thousand waters at once! Your great compassion
does not pass by a single creature. Steadily and
quietly the great ship of compassion sails over
the sea of sorrow.

From the Buddhist spiritual treatise Amidista

Repentance

Grandfather: look at our brokenness.
We know that in all creation
only the human family
has strayed from the Sacred Way.
We know that we are the ones
who are divided
and we are the ones
who must come back together
to walk in the Sacred Way.
Grandfather,
Sacred One,
teach us love, compassion and honour,
that we may heal the Earth
and heal each other.

Objibwa prayer, North America

Universal love

Even as a mother at the risk of her life would watch
over her own, her only child, so let us with boundless mind and goodwill survey the whole world.

Sutta-Nipata (from the Buddhist Pali canon)

Visions of a New World

Chapter Six

Visionary individuals of all races, cultures and faiths dare from time to time to dream of a better world – of global peace, an end to infant death from starvation, or more responsible energy use to limit environmental damage. But they wake from their dreams to a planet that is just as violent, poverty-stricken, polluted and brutal as ever. When things seem bleak, prayer can deliver hope that change is possible – that there is an alternative to the way things are.

Prayer challenges us to accept our responsibility. It empowers us to resist cruelty and injustice, filling us with compassion to work with all like-minded people for the relief of suffering. Crucially, prayer encourages steady action. We cannot solve all the world's problems in a sweeping moment of change. But our prayer lives can help us focus on taking the first step on the path to a new world. We may not necessarily see the end of what we start, but we will have set our descendants on the right path.

finding your vision

"I have a dream today," declared civil rights campaigner Martin Luther King in 1963. His celebrated vision – that "my four little children will one day live in a nation where they will not be judged by the colour of their skin but by the content of their character" – carried him to inspirational achievement in his campaign against racial injustice in the USA. It is no coincidence that King was a man of prayer – like others who have overcome seemingly insuperable odds in the cause of peace. Prayer inspired in him (and can inspire in us) a vision of a better world, and one that guides us in working to make that better world a reality.

He shall judge the poor with justice and defend the humble in the land with equity ... Then the wolf shall lie down with the sheep and the leopard with the kid.

Isaiah 11: 4, 6

We must cultivate our own vision. Read the testimonies and speeches of those who have acted as extraordinary catalysts for change – they inspire us by suggesting how ordinary people like you and I can remake ourselves as instruments of love and peace. Read also the biographies of people you especially admire. Make notes on the challenges they faced, and the resources they used to overcome them, and copy the most inspirational passages into your prayer journal.

In prayer make a conscious effort to envisage the utopian ideal for which you strive. Let us say that you are concerned about the treatment of refugees and migrants in Western countries: present the matter humbly as if before a divine tribunal, expressing as clearly as you can what you think is unjust and what should be done to improve the refugees' plight. Then envisage all these improvements achieved. Hold this vision: fix it in your mind. Pray that you may play a part in bringing reality closer to that ideal.

In seeking ways to put a vision into action, it can be helpful to focus on what we can achieve in small as well as large ways. We do not always see the consequences of our actions, and a small act of kindness or compassion may have positive effects beyond those that we witness. If you long to bring about a large-scale change but feel unable to make a difference, ask in prayer to change the focus of your vision. Try to see a part of your large plan that you can achieve quickly or easily. For example, if you are praying for an end to child poverty and exploitation, essentially you have the ambition that all children will be treated with compassion and respect. Set about achieving this at once with your own children or others you encounter in your daily life. Make a pledge, say, to offer time or support to a local youth group or reading scheme. Go out of your way to be respectful and helpful to children you meet.

Try also to cultivate a vision of yourself perfected. In prayer ask for help to see yourself as you could be if you moved beyond the fears and preconceptions that hold you back, achieving the lovingness that is your true inner nature. Return to this vision when you are at a low ebb: take strength from its goodness.

cultivating hope

Hope sustains our vision of a better world. The basis of hope is the certainty – acquired through prayer – that there is a power for good at work in the world. Mahatma Gandhi endured vilification and imprisonment during his nonviolent campaign against British rule in India, but was upheld by the confidence that right would triumph over wrong. He declared, "I can see that in the midst of death life persists, in the midst of untruth truth persists, in the midst of darkness light persists."

An effective way to cultivate hope is to focus repeatedly on heartening passages like this. Use them in meditation, repeating the words slowly in silence. In the place where you pray, frame and exhibit a text such as this, or the portrait of a figure such as Mother Teresa or Gandhi who reminds you of the power of hope.

Even in parts of the world where media reports concentrate on conflict and violence there are signs of hope. In Israel, there are more than sixty organizations (members of the Interreligious Coordinating Council) in which Jews and Muslims, Israelis and Arabs are working together for peace. I have met a group of rabbis (known as the Rabbis for Human Rights) who are defending  Palestinians from discrimination and have helped to rebuild Palestinians' homes damaged in the conflict. In northern India I have met Tibetan teenagers who walked for more than three months through the snowclad Himalayas to reach freedom. Repression cannot destroy the human capacity for hope.

exercise twenty-seven

launch hope

The word "hope" conjures up a whole spectrum of possible meanings. We might hope that a noisy neighbour will turn down the volume of his hi-fi system system. Then we might read in a newspaper of the hope that the deathtoll of an earthquake will be fewer than 1,000. All hopes in the world have their personal or domestic equivalents. Why not pray for hope in an outward spiral, starting with your own situation and fanning out to others?

1. Sit comfortably and locate the core of hope within yourself   the part of you that believes in good possibilities for yourself, your family, your friends, and for the world in general.

2. Now imagine yourself as a dove flying away from home, crossing borders, passing over other countries. As you fly you are gathering hope from your surroundings. How far do you have to travel before you reach an area of despair?

3. On reaching a trouble spot, imagine yourself dropping hope like bombs: the "hope-bombs" explode and send their benevolent contents to all those who believe that their situations are hopeless.

4. Reflect on the fact that the hope you desire for others is no different from the hope you enjoy at home. Pray for the outcomes that will justify your hope.

the healing of memories

In divided societies memories of past conflicts feed antagonisms between political factions or religious communities. Prayer, both individual and communal, offers a way forward, a chance to heal the bitter inheritance of the past.

As individuals we pray for peace. From time to time try making a conscious dedication of your prayer life to the healing of a conflict. Remember that in prayer we focus the resources of the divine to work *through us* for reconciliation. The medieval German Christian Meister Eckhart said, "The best attainment in life is to be still and let God act and speak in you." Stand-offs between factions may seem to be beyond our capacity to change, but it is astonishing how much individuals can achieve by, for example, trying always to turn away from hatred and aiming always to foster peace. In persevering with private prayer and in putting our prayers into action on a daily basis, we work for peace and the healing of memories in the best way we can as individuals.

Communal prayer can be a powerful agent for peace: the simple act of two communities coming together in fellowship promotes understanding. In some cases a ritual expression of penitence can be helpful. For example, people from both sides could be asked to attend an informal ceremony and write on a small piece of paper what they regret about their community's history. Organizers might then collect the pieces of paper and burn them to signify the purification of the past. Afterward, everyone

Hate is not conquered by hate: hate is conquered by love.

DHAMMAPADA
(BUDDHIST
SCRIPTURE)

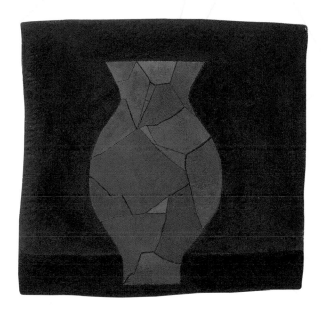

might join in singing or give one another a flower. Sometimes a formal apology on behalf of a community is a necessary step. A vital stage in building improved relations between Jews and Christians after the Holocaust was the Christians' apology for anti-Semitic teaching. When Pope John Paul II visited Jerusalem in March 2000, he inserted into the Western Wall a scroll confessing Christian complicity in the suffering of the Jews.

Ultimately the healing of memories depends on individuals' willingness to forgive. Nelson Mandela, the first president of the new multi-racial South Africa, set a magnificent example to his people: when he was released in 1990 after twenty-six years' imprisonment by the government, he declared that his mission was equally to captor and captive. Mandela even invited one of his jailers to be an honoured guest at the presidential inauguration.

the gifts of compassion

Through prayer we come to know that we are connected to all humanity. We discover the divine love that unites us with other people, love that naturally overflows in compassionate action to ease the pain of their suffering.

The Tibetan Buddhist practice of *tonglen* (Tibetan for "giving and taking") is a powerful way to develop and use compassion. Try *tonglen* in your prayer sessions. First focus on a suffering individual or group of people. Breathe in deeply and feel yourself drawing in all their emotional pain, right into your heart, making their grief your own. Then, when you breathe out, send love, warmth, kindness and compassion to the person or people who are suffering – replacing their fear and pain with equanimity, their misery with contentment or at least acceptance. When you first practise *tonglen* you may find yourself worrying that accepting others' suffering into your heart will harm you in some way. However, try to remember that your inner connection with the divine gives you immense strength to cope with the influx of pain.

You can perform *tonglen* for a friend, for a group of people such as famine victims, even for yourself – for example, if you feel frightened or blocked in your prayer life. When working for yourself in this way, try to visualize *two* selves – the suffering individual in the world and the higher, inner self that burns with divine love. Inhabit your higher self, drawing

When humanity is at one, God is One.

THE ZOHAR
(JEWISH MYSTICAL BOOK)

146

pain from and sending healing to your worldly self. Many people recommend performing *tonglen* for people you might encounter in the street or the subway. It might help to visualize the pain you breathe in as burning and dark, and the love you breathe out as a spreading white light.

Tonglen works directly against our natural tendency to block out others' suffering and to focus only on our own comfort. By developing our sense of connectedness with others, it undermines the assumption that we are helpless to act in the face of the world's suffering. Complement *tonglen* with practical action. Try making a pledge to express your compassion through a regular act of service in your community, such as helping in a centre for the homeless.

THE BODHISATTVA'S COMPASSION

In Buddhist teaching bodhisattvas are beings who have achieved enlightenment and so could escape the cycle of rebirth by entering *nirvana* (ultimate liberation), but whose compassion for other beings is so great that they choose to be reborn again and again in the world in order to help others. The bodhisattva's vow begins: "I take upon myself the burden of all suffering." Their magnanimity is an inspiration for those of us who are still far from enlightenment as we try to take practical, compassionate action for the relief of suffering in the world.

unity in all things

Many of us discover through our relationship with the divine a new sympathy with the Earth that inspires our efforts to protect it from exploitation. When, through prayer, we sense our connectedness with others, we also come to understand the intricate interdependence of all life, and the world as a gift that it is our duty to protect. The sense of global unity that burns more brightly in us as we go deeper into our prayer lives is both a responsibility and an enrichment.

Have you felt a shift in your attitude to animals and the Earth as you have been learning to pray? St Francis of Assisi and many other holy people of all faiths have had an intuitive sympathy with animals. The Jain religion teaches *ahimsa* or nonviolence toward all beings; Jains will not wear clothes made from animal products, and some Jain monks wear cloths over their mouths to prevent them from accidentally inhaling tiny insects.

Do you have pets? Perhaps you live in the country and have regular contact with animals. Think about how you treat them. Why not include your pets or other animals in your prayers? Think of animal species under threat of extinction: hold them and the precious Earth itself in the protective light of the divine.

You are part of the living Earth. Try taking a "prayer walk" through countryside or your local park: remind yourself that all you see — trees, grass, birds, dogs, people, clouds, even rain, sleet or snow if it is winter — is a manifestation of the divine, of its

flowering in the universe. You are part of that flowering. Skip ahead, perhaps run a few steps; and
give thanks. As you walk on, repeat under your
breath your chosen name for the divine.

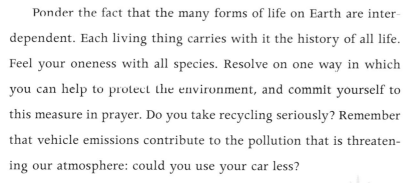

To develop a sense of oneness with the
Earth and its many species, practise the following mental visualization in the Earth's honour.
Imagine that you are looking at the planet from space:
notice the beauty and fragility of the globe bathed in sun-
light. Reflect on these words of the Soviet cosmonaut Aleksei
Leonov: "The Earth was small, light blue and so touchingly alone
... our home that must be defended like a holy relic."

Ponder the fact that the many forms of life on Earth are inter-
dependent. Each living thing carries with it the history of all life.
Feel your oneness with all species. Resolve on one way in which
you can help to protect the environment, and commit yourself to
this measure in prayer. Do you take recycling seriously? Remember
that vehicle emissions contribute to the pollution that is threaten-
ing our atmosphere: could you use your car less?

Recognize that from space we see the planet as a whole – we do
not see differences between nations, peoples and religions. Ask the
divine, in words prayed in space on the Apollo Eight mission in
1967, to "show us what each of us can do to set forth the coming
of the day of universal peace."

the foundation of fellowship

*O God of many
names,
Lover of
all people,
Give peace
in our hearts,
in our homes,
in our world,
in our universe:
The peace of
our need,
the peace of
your will.*

GEORGE
APPLETON
(1902–1993)

Growing awareness of our unity with all beings helps to harmonize us with people of different faiths in the search for universal peace and reconciliation. To mark the new millennium, in August 2000, one thousand religious and spiritual leaders gathered in the General Assembly Hall of the United Nations and for nearly four hours offered prayers, in many languages and from most religious traditions, for the peace of the world.

If you plan to arrange "interfaith" prayers in your area, you have a number of options. Sometimes a member of one faith is invited as a guest to another faith's place of worship and asked to give an address, or say a prayer; or members of each faith in turn might offer prayers while the others listen; while a third option is to agree a common order of proceedings and invite all present to share in saying some prayers and an affirmation together.

Prayer awakens us to the certainty of a spiritual unity that transcends differences between religions. Experiencing the prayers of another religious tradition can be liberating, helping us to focus on the most fundamental values. The final decades of the twentieth century saw a number of official interfaith initiatives. In 1990, for example, a group of Jews travelled to the Dalai Lama's base in Dharamsala, northern India, for an unprecedented religious dialogue between Judaism and Tibetan Buddhism that participants reported was illuminating on both sides. Each of us can participate in this journey of interfaith discovery in the quiet

of our own homes. There are several excellent anthologies of prayers, some of which are listed in the bibliography of this book, that draw on the religious traditions of the world. Most bookshops today have large sections devoted to spirituality.

Pray in any way that feels right, in the certainty that the divine will hear you no matter how you communicate. If you find it helpful, quarry the world's religious traditions for prayers, dedications, songs, meditation practices, mystical writings, ceremonies, icons and statues that you can use in your own prayer life. The wisest words and practices point beyond themselves to the divine, the uncontainable mystery in which we find ultimate meaning and inspiring compassion for ourselves, our fellow humans, our fellow species – and for all life.

visionary words and deeds

In death life persists

Whilst everything around me is ever-changing, ever-dying, there is underlying all that changes a living power that is changeless, that holds all together, that creates, dissolves, and re-creates. That informing power or spirit is God ... In the midst of death life persists, in the midst of untruth truth persists, in the midst of darkness light persists. Hence I gather that God is life, truth, light. God is love. God is the supreme good ... I know that I can do nothing. God can do everything. O God, make me your fit instrument and use me as you will.

*Mahatma Gandhi (1869–1948), Indian nationalist
leader and holy man*

Love is the only bridge

Our Father, help us to know the light-year distance between one planet and another. Yet help us to know that the distance between one race and another can be even wider. Lead us to know the ancient wisdom that love is the only bridge between peoples, nations and universes.

Hawaiian prayer

Two prayers of loving service

I sought my God,

my God I could not see;

I sought my soul,

my soul eluded me;

I sought my brother,

and I found all three.

Anon.

By love may He be gotten and holden, by

thought never.

Julian of Norwich (c.1342–c.1413), English mystic

The sacred hoop

I was seeing in a sacred manner the shapes of all
things in the spirit, and the shape of all shapes as
they must live together like one being. And I saw
that the sacred hoop of my people was one of many
hoops that made one circle, wide as daylight and as
starlight, and in the centre grew one mighty flowering tree to shelter all the children of one mother
and one father. And I saw that it was holy.

Black Elk, Native American spiritual leader

Let there be peace on Earth

Let the time come, O God, when there shall be
peace on Earth, brotherhood among races, freedom from
fear and freedom from war, freedom to think and speak
at the dictates of conscience, when our systems of justice
shall be protective and healing and all people live in a
world that is closer to the principles of your kingdom.

George Appleton (1902–1993), English bishop

Universal peace

May there be peace in the higher regions;
may there be peace in the firmament;
may there be peace on Earth.
May the waters flow peacefully;
may the herbs and plants grow peacefully;
may all the living powers bring unto us peace.
The supreme Lord is peace.
May we all be in peace, peace, and only peace;
and may that peace come unto each of us.
Shanti, shanti, shanti.

*Note: "Shanti" (an ancient Sanskrit word) can be loosely
translated into English as "peace", but its true meaning is
more accurately conveyed in "peace beyond understanding".*

The Vedas *(ancient Hindu scripture)*

Litany of peace

As we are together, praying for peace, let us be
truly with each other.

Let us be at peace within ourselves, our bodies and
our minds, our emotions and spirit.

Let us return to ourselves and become wholly
ourselves.

Let us be aware of the source of being common to
us and to all living things.

Evoking the presence of the Great Compassion, let
us open our hearts to receive compassion – for
ourselves and for all living beings.

Let us pray that all living beings may realize that
they are all brothers and sisters, all nourished
from the same source of life.

Let us pray that we ourselves may cease to be the
cause of suffering to each other.

Let us pledge ourselves to live in a way which will
not deprive other beings of air, water, food,
shelter, or the chance to live.

With humility, with awareness of the uniqueness of
life, and with compassion for the suffering
around us, let us pray for the establishment of
peace in our hearts and peace on Earth.

Based on a Buddhist meditation

further reading

ADAM, DAVID. *The Edge of Glory*, SPCK, London, 1985; Morehouse Publishing, Harrisburg, Pennsylvania, 1992.

APPLETON, GEORGE, ed. *The Oxford Book of Prayer*, Oxford University Press, Oxford, 1985; Oxford University Press, New York, 1989.

BOUX, DOROTHY. *The Golden Thread: Words of Hope for a Changing World*, Shepheard-Walwyn, London and Gateway Books, Bath, 1990; Fulcrum Publishing, Colorado, 1995.

CARDEN, JOHN. *Morning, Noon and Night: Prayers and Meditations from the Third World*, Church Missionary Society, London, 1976.

CLARK, SUSAN J. *Celebrating Earth Holy Days: A Resource Guide for Faith Communities*, Crossroad Publishing, New York, 1992.

CRAGG, KENNETH. *Alive to God*, Oxford University Press, Oxford, 1970.

DALAI LAMA (TENZIN GYATSO). *The Dalai Lama's Book of Daily Meditations: The Path to Tranquillity*, Viking Press, New York, 1999; Rider, London, 2000.

FAIVRE, DANIEL, ed. *Resources for Multifaith Celebrations*, Westminster Interfaith, London, 1997.

GHOSANANDA, MAHA. *Step by Step: Meditations on Wisdom and Compassion*, Parallax Press, Berkeley, California, 1992.

GOLLANCZ, VICTOR. *A Year of Grace* (1955) and *The New Year of Grace* (1962), Victor Gollancz, London 1955 and 1962.

GREENE, BARBARA AND GOLLANCZ, VICTOR, eds. *God of a Hundred Names*, Victor Gollancz, London, 1962.

GRIFFITHS, BEDE. *Universal Wisdom: A Journey Through the Sacred Literature of the World*, HarperCollins, London, 1994.

HAPPOLD, F. C. *Mysticism: a Study and an Anthology*, Penguin Books, London, 1963; Viking Press, New York, 1991.

HARCOURT, GILES. *Dawn Through Our Darkness*, Collins, London, 1985.

POTTER, JEAN AND BRAYBROOKE, MARCUS, eds. *All in Good Faith, A Resource Book for Multi-Faith Prayer*, World Congress of Faiths, Oxford and CoNexus Press, Ada, Michigan, 1997.

ROBERTS, ELIZABETH AND AMIDON, ELIAS, eds. *Earth Prayers from Around the World*, Harper, San Francisco, California, 1991.

SATCHIDANANDA, SRI SWAMI. *The Lotus Prayer Book*, Integral Yoga Publications, Buckingham, Virginia, 1986.

TERESA, MOTHER. *Everything Starts From Prayer*, White Cloud Press, Ashland, Oregon, 1998.

THICH NHAT HANH. *Being Peace*, Parallax Press, Berkeley, California, 1987.

WHITTAKER, AGNES. *All in the End is Harvest: an Anthology for Those who Grieve*, Darton, Longman and Todd, London, 1984.

WILSON ANDREW, ed. *World Scripture, A Comparative Anthology of Sacred Texts*, Paragon House, New York, 1991.

index

acknowledgments

The Publishers wish to thank the following for their kind permission to reproduce prayers in this book.

Yoga Publications, Yogaville, Virginia, US for prayers from *The Lotus Prayer Book* (1986): pages 33 (I will sing you a song, Our Lord fills every heart), 35 (Prayer for all beings), 57 (God's Answer), 58 (Grant me the ability to be alone), 136 (Mother of the universe), 137 (Universal love), 152 (In death life persists), 154 (Universal peace)

Rachel Bennett and the Oxford University Press for prayers from *The Oxford Book of Prayer*, ed. George Appleton (1985): pages 32 (O clearness beyond measure), 34 (May the road rise to meet you), 58 (Help me to feel your presence), 59 (Keep me straight, God is the journey and the journey's end), 81 (Peace prayer)

Rachel Bennett and SPCK for prayers from *Jerusalem Prayers*, ed. George Appleton (1974): pages 80 (For quiet hearts), 134 (Your eyes of compassion), 154 (Let there be peace on Earth)

Rev. John Carden and the CMS for prayers from *Morning, Noon and Night* (1976) on page 111 (Four prayers from China) and Rev. John Carden and SPCK for prayers from *Another Day* (1986): pages 136 (The great ship of compassion), 137 (Repentance), 152 (Love is the only bridge)

David Adam and SPCK for prayers from *The Edge of Glory* (1985): pages 34 (Deep peace of the running wave), 78 (Stilling the body)

Rev. Giles Harcourt for prayer from *Dawn through our Darkness* (1985) on page 109 (Harmony with the divine)

The World Congress of Faiths for prayers from *All in Good Faith* (1997), ed. Jean Potter and Marcus Braybrooke: pages 79 (Waiting on God), 110 (Sacred Earth), 111 (An all-embracing love), 134 (For my sake), 153 (The sacred hoop), 155 (Litany of peace)

Every effort has been made to obtain permission for copyright material. The Publishers and the Author apologize for any omissions, which are wholly unintentional. They will, if informed, make any necessary corrections in future editions of this book.